INVESTIGATING ARTIFACTS

Making Masks, Creating Myths, Exploring Middens
teacher's guide

Grades
Kindergarten–6

Skills
Observing, Recording, Sorting and Classifying, Finding and Making Patterns, Mapping and Diagramming, Making Inferences, Designing Models, Writing, Relating, Communicating, Drama and Role-Playing, Working Cooperatively, Analyzing Data

Concepts
Anthropology; Archaeology; Cultural Diversity and Similarity; Art, Language, and Culture; Myths, Legends, and Storytelling

Science Themes
Patterns of Change, Models & Simulations, Systems & Interactions, Structure, Scale, Unity & Diversity

Mathematics Strands
Logic, Pattern, Functions, Measurement, Number

Nature of Science and Mathematics
Changing Nature of Facts and Theories, Cooperative Efforts, Scientific Community, Real-Life Applications, Interdisciplinary, Creativity and Constraints

Katharine Barrett
Lincoln Bergman
Gigi Dornfest
Linda Lipner
Carolyn Willard

LHS GEMS

Great Explorations in Math and Science (GEMS)
Lawrence Hall of Science
University of California at Berkeley

Cover Design and Illustrations
Lisa Klofkorn

Photographs
Richard Hoyt

Lawrence Hall of Science, University of California, Berkeley, CA 94720.

Chairman: Glenn T. Seaborg
Director: Marian C. Diamond

Publication of *Investigating Artifacts* was made possible by a grant from the McDonnell Douglas Foundation and the McDonnell Douglas Employees Community Fund. The GEMS project and the Lawrence Hall of Science greatly appreciate this support.

Initial support for the origination and publication of the GEMS series was provided by the A.W. Mellon Foundation and the Carnegie Corporation of New York. GEMS has also received support from the McDonnell-Douglas Foundation and the McDonnell-Douglas Employees Community Fund, the Hewlett Packard Foundation, and the people at Chevron USA. GEMS also gratefully acknowledges the contribution of word processing equipment from Apple Computer, Inc. This support does not imply responsibility for statements or views expressed in publications of the GEMS program. Under a grant from the National Science Foundation, GEMS Leader's Workshops have been held across the country. For further information on GEMS leadership opportunities, or to receive a publication brochure and the *GEMS Network News*, please contact GEMS at the address and phone number below.

International Standard Book Number: 0-912511-82-6

COMMENTS WELCOME

Great Explorations in Math and Science (GEMS) is an ongoing curriculum development project. GEMS guides are revised periodically, to incorporate teacher comments and new approaches. We welcome your criticisms, suggestions, helpful hints, and any anecdotes about your experience presenting GEMS activities. Your suggestions will be reviewed each time a GEMS guide is revised. Please send your comments to: GEMS Revisions, c/o Lawrence Hall of Science, University of California, Berkeley, CA 94720.
The phone number is (415) 642-7771.

Great Explorations in Math and Science (GEMS) Program

The Lawrence Hall of Science (LHS) is a public science center on the University of California at Berkeley campus. LHS offers a full program of activities for the public, including workshops and classes, exhibits, films, lectures, and special events. LHS is also a center for teacher education and curriculum research and development.

Over the years, LHS staff have developed a multitude of activities, assembly programs, classes, and interactive exhibits. These programs have proven to be successful at the Hall and should be useful to schools, other science centers, museums, and community groups. A number of these guided-discovery activities have been published under the Great Explorations in Math and Science (GEMS) title, after an extensive refinement process that includes classroom testing of trial versions, modifications to ensure the use of easy-to-obtain materials, and carefully written and edited step-by-step instructions and background information to allow presentation by teachers without special background in mathematics or science.

Staff
Glenn T. Seaborg, **Principal Investigator**
Jacqueline Barber, **Director**
Cary Sneider, **Curriculum Specialist**
Katharine Barrett, John Erickson, Jaine Kopp, Kimi Hosoume, Laura Lowell, Linda Lipner, Laura Tucker, Carolyn Willard, **Staff Development Specialists**
Jan M. Goodman, **Mathematics Consultant**
Cynthia Ashley, **Administrative Coordinator**
Gabriela Solomon, **Distribution Coordinator**
Lisa Haderlie Baker, **Art Director**
Carol Bevilacqua and Lisa Klofkorn, **Designers**
Lincoln Bergman, **Principal Editor**
Carl Babcock and Kay Fairwell, **Associate Editors**

Contributing Authors

Jacqueline Barber	Jan M. Goodman
Katharine Barrett	Alan Gould
Lincoln Bergman	Kimi Hosoume
Jaine Kopp	Sue Jagoda
Linda Lipner	Larry Malone
Laura Lowell	Cary I. Sneider
Linda De Lucchi	Jennifer Meux White
Jean Echols	Carolyn Willard

Reviewers

We would like to thank the following educators who reviewed, tested, or coordinated the reviewing of this series of GEMS materials in manuscript and draft form. Their critical comments and recommendations, based on presentation of these activities in classrooms nationwide, contributed significantly to these GEMS publications. Their participation in the review process does not necessarily imply endorsement of the GEMS program or responsibility for statements or views expressed in these publications. Their role is an invaluable one, and their feedback is carefully recorded and integrated as appropriate into the publications. Thank You!

ALASKA
Coordinator: **Cynthia Dolmas Curran**

Iditarod Elementary, Wasilla
    Mary Helen Cole
    Cynthia Dolmas Curran
    Michael J. Curran
    Jana Schlereth DePriest
    Ruth Felberg
    Deborah Waisanen

CALIFORNIA

GEMS Center, Huntington Beach
Coordinator: **Susan Spoeneman**

Circle View Elementary School, Huntington Beach
    Mary R. Berrier
    Stan Carroll
    Alice R. French
    Anita Fuller
    Marilyn Wilton
    Amy Yoshihara

William E. Kettler Elementary School, Huntington Beach
    JoAnne Smith Berg
    Kay Fletcher
    Patricia Gates
    Elaine Goodnoe
    Sandy Harrell

San Francisco Bay Area
Coordinator: **Cynthia Ashley**

Edison Elementary School, Alameda
    Jane Baldi
    Barbara Klaasen
    Sandra Downey

Foothill Elementary School, Pittsburg
    Gary Diaz, Coordinator
    Gail Caruso
    Gisele Cassidy-Phillips
    Iris Contreras
    Annie H. Clawson
    Susan M. Luoni
    Fran Marshack
    David Rose
    Sol Rosenshein
    Nadine Seedall

Franklin Elementary School, Berkeley
    Katherine Lunine
    Scott Wachenheim
    Mario Zelaya

Glassbrook Elementary School, Hayward
    Marianne Camp
    Laura Suzanne Clark
    Patricia Anne Geary
    Marina Xavier

Lincoln Elementary School, Newark
    Linda Agler
    Midge Fuller
    Beverly Hall
    Judy Levenson

Los Medanos Elementary School, Pittsburg
    Sandi Dias
    Cheryl Duran
    Paula McNally
    Mary Pino
    Linda Switzer

Martin Luther King Jr. Junior High School, Berkeley
    Phoebe Tanner

Oxford Elementary School, Berkeley
Joseph Brulenski
Carole Bennett Simmons
Janet Levenson
Kathy Rashidi

Park Day School, Oakland
Karen Corzan
Catharine Keyes
Susan McLean
Joan Wright-Albertini

Peralta Year Round Elementary School, Oakland
Elizabeth A. Bandy
Paulette Besse
M. Anne Larsen

Sierra School, El Cerrito
Laurie Chandler
Gail Gundelach
Phil Gilsenan
Harry Lackritz Gray
Janie Havemeyer

Washington Elementary School, Berkeley
Carolyn R. Adams
Rita Davies
Diane Meltzer
Patricia Ungern

GEORGIA
Coordinator: **Yonnie Carol Pope**

Mountain View Elementary, Marietta
Robin M. DeVaux
Cathy Howell
Ruth Lang
Diane Pine Miller
Samantha Marie Miller
Yonnie Carol Pope
Barbara Smoot
Denise Langston Thomas
Kimberly L. West

KENTUCKY
Coordinator: **Dee Moore**

St. Joseph School, Louisville
Kathy Fensterer
Diane Flechler
Mary Jane Mascarich
Barbara Smoot
Theresa Watson

Simpsonville Elementary School, Louisville
Sheryl Block
Brenda Breidert
Elizabeth C. Brown
Paula Smith

TEXAS
Coordinators: **Melanie Lewis** and **Sarah Fogg**

Deep Wood Elementary School, Round Rock
Kathy Culpepper
Lana Culver
Carol Hernandez
Sandra Mouldin
Marilyn F. Sutch
Julia Swain
Sherry Wilkison

WASHINGTON
Coordinator: **Scott Stowell**

Bemiss Elementary School, Spokane
Cindy Beard
Brenda Fuglevand
Shelly Fuller
Margaret A. Haines
Patricia Moen

Longfellow Elementary School, Spokane
Joy Chastek
Birgit Gorman
Cris Welch
Sandra Westerman

Acknowledgments

This book owes its existence to a fortunate and collaborative weave of people and circumstance. The authors are pleased at the way their cooperative process and the interdisciplinary nature and content of the activities and content built upon and strengthened each other. GEMS Director Jacqueline Barber had the original vision of weaving the three main activities together.

We would particularly like to thank Rosemary Ackerley Christiansen, of the Ojibwe Mekana Curriculum Materials Laboratory in Duluth Minnesota for her incisive critique of this unit, posing several major areas of cultural and pedagogical concern, and raising questions relating to the use of the terms "Native American" and "myth." Lee Sprague, of the Chippewa, Ottowa, and Potawatomi United Nation, who has served as an educational consultant on previous LHS projects, also reviewed the manuscript and made important suggestions for improvement. We are indebted as well to Joan La France, who read an earlier version, made several major comments and recommended other consultants. We hope that at least some small portion of the wisdom and information these consultants communicated is represented in these activities. Of course, the final responsibility for this guide and its content rests with the authors. We are all agreed that more and better teachings and learnings on the ways of life of these "First Nations," will hopefully, in the words of Rosemary Christensen, "help us all enormously as we struggle to find a way to learn about each other outside of war-type behavior."

The "Masks" activities in this unit derive from similar activities that were originated by Joseph Brulenski, a teacher at Oxford Elementary School in Berkeley, whose class appears in several of the photographs in this guide. Originally designed as a creative way to allow for students of all economic backgrounds to take part in traditional schoolwide Halloween festivities (not just those whose parents could afford fancy costumes) the "Masks" activities soon lent themselves to wonderful artistic, cross-cultural and mathematical explorations. They were further developed by Linda Lipner, Director of the Math Education Department at Lawrence Hall of Science (LHS) and other staff members who taught classes at the Hall.

The "Myths" portion was developed especially for this unit by Carolyn Willard, a GEMS Staff Development Specialist. One of her early inspirations was a similar myth-related modeling activity in the GEMS guide *Earth, Moon, and Stars*, written by Cary Sneider. Carolyn also immersed herself in numerous books chronicling the spiritual beliefs and stories of Native peoples in the Americas and beyond, and played a leading role in bringing together the entire unit, by producing the local trial version, incorporating teacher comments following national testing, and helping develop the special resource pages.

The story "How the Stars Came to Be" was first told to us by Kevin Beals, a teacher in the LHS Chemistry Education Department. We continue to research its origin. Marian Drabkin, the LHS Librarian, shared her extensive knowledge about and collection of folklore, especially as we developed the resource pages for the myths portion. The GEMS project is developing a handbook detailing young people's literature connections to the GEMS series and the consultant on that project, Valerie Wheat, also provided valuable assistance to the authors of this guide.

Katharine Barrett, Director of the Biology Education Department, and Gigi Dornfest, a teacher in that department, were the main authors of the "Middens" portion of this unit. Basing their work on numerous archaeological activities that have been presented at LHS, they displayed great flexibility and originality in adapting the activities to the school classroom, originating the role play activity, and providing different options for students of varying ages and abilities to find out "what is hidden in their midden." We also want to thank Wade Barrett for the use of the map he made when investigating his midden.

Cynthia Ashley coordinated the local and national testing process. She was aided by a number of dedicated assistants, including Nancy Kedzierski, Felicia Roston, Vivian Tong, and Stephanie Van Meter. The teachers who presented these activities in the classroom are listed elsewhere in this guide. As always, we thank both them and their students for many important suggestions and refinements.

The GEMS Principal Editor, Lincoln Bergman, also played a major role in weaving this unit together and worked with consultants to be sensitive to the complex issues involved. He produced the national trial version of the unit, incorporating staff and teacher comment from local trial testing, and is the primary author of the introductory and background sections. He is also the author of the poem on page 32 that is inspired by a Huron creation myth.

Contents

Introduction

Although they overlap, there is a distinction between anthropology and archaeology. Anthropologists study the origins and physical and cultural development of all humanity, past and present. Archaeologists study past peoples and their cultures by analysis of artifacts, especially those that have been excavated. Archaeology must also be differentiated from paleontology, which is generally the study of ancient life, such as dinosaurs and other early life forms, rather than human cultures. A listing of some of the many excellent resources on these subjects is included near the end of this guide.

We have occasionally been asked, in regard to this guide, "Where's the science?" or "Where's the math?" Without investigation, some may suppose that because there is much multicultural, literary, and artistic richness in this guide, there is less science and math. Nothing could be farther from the truth! The sorting and classification component of the masks activities is central to the development of these important skills in both mathematics and science. Archaeology itself is a longstanding and highly respected discipline that makes use of many scientific and mathematical skills, processes, and concepts. Its close relative, anthropology, also has many scientific aspects. Efforts to explain the natural world as represented in human myths can be compared to the quest of science, and can help students understand more about the very nature of science. The distinction between evidence and inference and emphasis on logical reasoning that are central to all three of the main activities in this guide are also key elements in both the scientific method and mathematical problem-solving. Finally, all of the above, combined with the ecological and folk wisdom found in Native American and world cultures, can give students an appreciation for diversity, and of the ways science and mathematics relate to and intersect with society and social issues. Where's the math? Where's the science? It's powerfully interwoven throughout Investigating Artifacts!

This guide interweaves three exciting activities with major themes in science and the humanities. Drawing respectfully upon the deep, diverse, and living folkways of Native American cultures, these activities can help provide students with a wider understanding of the world around them and a greater appreciation for cultural diversity.

The unit integrates science, mathematics, art, language arts and social science. Students are introduced to essential elements of anthropology and archaeology. They begin to understand the importance and the pleasure of retrieving information that might otherwise be lost forever. Students learn the value of understanding and appreciating past civilizations as well as of inheriting and conserving ancient wisdom that we can use today. Their own hands-on activities connect the past to the present, and provide perspectives on our own modern ways of life.

Important skills, concepts, and themes in science and mathematics run like brightly-colored threads through the entire unit. Language arts activities and extensions add their brilliant hues, with free and full expression of artistic creativity and imagination strongly encouraged. The connecting thread of examining and evaluating objects and evidence, and drawing inferences from often limited, uneven, or disparate information, unites all the sciences and can be one of your students' most important areas of intellectual growth and development during this unit.

The larger social science and multicultural education issues introduced by learning more about past and present Native American cultures, histories, and current realities are at the heart of this guide. Please read through the "Background for Teachers" section on page 70 for more perspective on this vitally important subject, and for additional information on other components of this unit, including archaeology.

Many teachers have found it helpful to read out loud at least three or four Native American myths in the weeks before beginning this unit. This not only establishes a storytelling mood and framework, but also acquaints younger students with the kind of story they are asked to create during Sessions 3 and 4. Or you may want to schedule a few sorting and classification activities in the weeks before the first two sessions. You could also consider variations in order of presentation, depending on student experience and your own inclinations. You, of course, are best able to evaluate the backgrounds, skills, abilities, and prior experiences of your class.

The unit has also been presented starting with the "Myths" sessions, but because so much of the unit relates to the natural world, and because direct physical contact aids understanding of abstract ideas, we begin this guide with the nature walk and the hands-on creation of masks.

Making Natural Masks

In the past and in the present, people of all cultures have used masks for a wide variety of reasons, from the sacred and ceremonial to the humorous and playful. Native Americans from many tribes and nations use masks made of natural materials and objects. Sessions 1 and 2 introduce the fascinating and revealing subject of masks, while at the same time emphasizing key skills in mathematics and the sciences.

It is important to note, as the guide endeavors to do, that in some cultures certain masks are very sacred and secret ceremonial objects, to be viewed only by the initiates of that culture. In making maskmaking a joyful class activity, we do not in any way intend to diminish or show any disrespect for this more serious side of masks.

In the course of gathering the natural materials for their masks, your students gain additional understandings about which materials are natural and which are not. In this activity, and the myth-making activity to follow, students are asked to imagine themselves to be living in the days of long-ago Native Americans, and they get to take a walk outside to explore and gather objects from their environment.

After enjoying ample free exploration of the objects, the students sort them into two categories of their own choice. It is made clear that there are many ways to sort, and no "right" or "wrong" way to perform this task. After reporting on this and subsequent ways of sorting, the class plays a "Secret Sort" game.

In Session 2, students use the objects and materials they gathered to create masks. Creativity comes into full play and observation skills are refined, as students make simple inferences from the masks and draw some conclusions about the world around them. They can use the masks in a variety of activities, including sorting and classification, writing and drama. Depending on your preference and student enthusiasm, the mask each student creates can become part of the myth-making in the next two sessions, physically bridging the unit.

The term "myth" is discussed in greater detail in the background section. It is meant throughout this unit as: an oral narrative, story, or legend that over time has become so important in a particular people's culture that it becomes part of their spiritual belief or social value system, or an explanation or metaphor for the natural world. In this sense, the Greek, Roman, or Nordic legends and deities, the literature of the world's religions, and many of the oral narratives of Native peoples all around the world can be called "myths." It is thus meant very respectfully. However, some reviewers of this unit consider the term negative or inadequate. If you are concerned that the word myth does a disservice or is disrespectful due to its common other meaning, which implies falsehood, then feel free to use other words and your own explanations. Especially with younger students you could avoid confusion by using the word "story" or perhaps "special story."

Creating Myths

In the next two sessions of this guide, students are introduced to myths as ways in which ancient people helped explain the world around them. They learn that one of the ways to find out more about a culture, past or present, is through studying their myths, which can provide clues to the way people live. In Session 3, students imagine themselves to be in the area where they live, only at a time long ago, when no people except Native Americans lived there. In teams of two, students draw pictures, write down stories, or do both, to create a story that explains observations of the sun, the moon, the stars, animal behavior, or the weather. With younger students, you may want to select only one of these options, such as the movement of the Sun, again depending on their experience.

During Session 4, students share their drawings and stories with each other. The teacher relates a Native American story explaining the origin of night and day, then the class discusses the way myths reflect the cultures they come from, and how myths relate to science.

In addition to the broader cultural aspects of student myth-making, this activity helps hone process skills such as observing, recording, generating theories, distinguishing between observation and inference, and designing models. It can also whet student curiosity about the sun, moon, stars and the natural world. So far in this unit, the students have created a concrete cultural object, their mask, and used the power of their own and their partner's imaginations to create myths as theories about natural phenomena. With insights gained from both activities, they now work cooperatively in teams to investigate artifacts of the past.

What's Hidden in the Midden?

In Sessions 5 and 6 students are introduced to a series of activities that model the work of archaeologists and the studies of anthropologists as they investigate the past. A "midden" is defined as a place where people have left things. Instead of investigating a midden at an archaeological dig, students are given middens in the classroom, made from shoe boxes or similar containers. Inside the midden are various layers of earth representing different time periods. In the layers are artifacts and materials that provide clues to the past.

There is a substantial amount of time involved in constructing the middens. Careful, step-by-step instructions are provided and many teachers have wisely recruited parent volunteers. Despite the amount of preparation, the most frequent teacher response has been "it was worth it!" The level of student interest, enthusiasm, and continued involvement is extremely high. As one young student put it, "Can we do this again?...for 100 minutes!"

Students learn techniques for sifting, removing, keeping track of, analyzing, and classifying the contents of the midden. Working in teams, students make maps of their middens and attempt to draw conclusions about the simulated artifacts they find. They refine skills related to not only archaeology and anthropology, but all science and mathematics: observation, recording, sorting, classification, mapping, making inferences, and drawing conclusions. Depending on your students' grade level and prior experiences, several alternative approaches are offered, including a possible grid system.

"Going Further" activities can explore the issues raised by anthropological investigations of specific Native American structures and cultures, or by land development projects that encroach upon sites sacred to the Native peoples of a particular region. Other activities could include student investigation of modern garbage to draw some conclusions about present-day culture and to consider the importance of recycling and other conservation measures.

It is important to note that there are laws relating to situations that arise when, for example, a contractor is excavating land in preparation for a new structure, and cultural artifacts or burial sites are uncovered. For all students, you can communicate the idea that there are reasons why it may not be acceptable to proceed with either an archaeological excavation or a construction project. For older students, if you want to make sure these key ethical issues are raised, we suggest a scenario for the middens activity that includes these concerns. See #2 in the "Going Further" activities listed on page 63, and other marginal notes throughout the middens activity, or devise your own approach to these issues.

Weaving It All Together

While each of these activities is involving and rewarding in itself, it is also true that "the whole is greater than the sum of its parts." The cumulative impact of the three main activities is to widen cultural understanding and encourage creativity, as well as to refine and reinforce science and mathematics skills. For upper elementary students emphasis can be placed on the scientific thinking process of "making inferences and drawing conclusions" which can include a process of mental reasoning, with a careful weighing of evidence and variables. While the more complex and abstract aspects of making inferences are often considered more appropriate for higher grade levels, intriguing investigative activities like these set an excellent stage for more elementary introductions to simple inferences and the evaluation of evidence. When interwoven with free exploration, art, and literature, the positive benefits echo throughout the curriculum and speak to the "whole" student.

The distinctive histories, cultures, and present-day realities of Native Americans are the natural fiber whose weave gives this unit strength and vitality. If it should happen that there are children of Native American backgrounds in your class, or if you can make contact with a local Indian community or educational organization, by all means encourage direct classroom involvement and consultation in whatever ways seem best.

Like beautiful Native American blankets or belts, like the quilted fabrics that are so integral a part of popular cultures the world over, this unit can be woven together in imaginative and creative ways. It is our hope that these activities, when enlivened by the creative powers of students and teachers in the classroom, will provide many educational opportunities and a truly memorable learning experience.

everal of the people who reviewed this guide from the perspective of Native people raised issues related to archaeology. As one reviewer put it, "For the past several years, Tribal people have spent an enormous amount of time trying to convince non-Tribal people to quit bothering Tribal sacred sites." While reverence for ancestors and the passing on of lessons from the past through spiritual practice, native language, and storytelling is highly valued, the digging up of the past, in order to analyze pieces of it, can be viewed as contrary to Tribal beliefs, values and traditions. This can be seen as especially negative when that "unearthing" is done by people outside of the culture involved, who may view it as a novelty, romanticize it, be motivated by financial profit, or be disrespectful in other ways. The "Going Further" activities for Sessions 5 and 6 about what happens when a shopping mall project unearths a sacred site relate to a small extent to these issues. You may want to widen the discussion by having students research and debate or role-play differing points of view about both archaeology and anthropology and their relationship to the peoples and cultures they study. One recommended adult book on this subject is *Savigism and Civilization: A Study of the Indian and American Mind* by Roy Harvey Pearce, University of California Press, Los Angeles, 1988.

It is well worth noting, that, given the historical fact of the massive death and destruction caused by European expansion, some anthropologists and archaeologists have made very important contributions to the preservation of and revived respect for Native American cultural achievements. Student understanding of and respect for different cultures can help create more such sensitive scholars in the future!

Time Frame

As mentioned in the Introduction, many teachers have found it helpful to read Native American stories to the class in the weeks before beginning this unit, as well as during the unit. This familiarizes students with the kind of story they are asked to create during Sessions 3 and 4, and sets a positive, storytelling mood that can help tie together the whole unit. For suggestions of stories to read, see the "Native American Myths Resource Page" on page 39, check the longer list on page 77, or start by reading the stories we have included in Sessions 3 and 4.

Session 1: Natural Collecting and Sorting
Teacher Preparation: 30 minutes
Classroom Activity: One or two 45–60 minute sessions

Session 2: Making Masks and Inferences
Teacher Preparation: 30–60 minutes
Classroom Activity: One or two 45–60 minute sessions

Session 3: Creating Myths
Teacher Preparation: 30–60 minutes
Classroom Activity: One or two 45–60 minute sessions

Session 4: Sharing Myths
Teacher Preparation: 15 minutes
Classroom Activity: 45–60 minutes

Session 5: Uncovering the Past: What's Hidden in the Midden?
Teacher Preparation: 2 to 5 hours (first time)
        1 1/2 hours (subsequent presentations)
Classroom Activity: One or two 60-minute sessions
(Preparation time can be significantly reduced with help. See page 45)

Session 6: Putting Together Clues From the Past
Teacher Preparation: 15 minutes
Classroom Activity: 45–60 minutes

Note: Fall is a Good Time to Begin this Unit

It is possible to teach this unit successfully at any time of the year. Many teachers recommend beginning the unit in the fall, if possible. Quite often, the fall curriculum includes teaching about early cultures, which makes this the best time to integrate these activities with social studies. Since the first activity involves a walk to gather natural objects, autumn is a time when natural materials such as leaves, twigs, seeds, etc. can be found easily on the ground. (You'll probably want to avoid scheduling this first activity during the winter, especially if you live in a cold climate.) Fall may also be preferable to Spring for the first activity because plants are less likely to be producing pollen then, thus avoiding possible problems with springtime allergies.

Session 1: Natural Collecting and Sorting

Overview

n this session, students go on a walk in the school neighborhood. They collect natural objects that they find, and sort the objects in many different ways. Then they make simple inferences and draw conclusions about their neighborhood. The activities are designed to allow students to make discoveries and observations, develop attribute vocabulary, practice sorting and classification skills, and work collaboratively. It also serves as an exciting and appropriate opening to the entire unit, which focuses on the ways ancient and modern peoples create art from and seek to explain the natural world around them.

In the next session, students use the materials they gathered to make masks, observe patterns among the masks, and make inferences about the possible uses of the masks. The activities in both sessions integrate science, mathematics, art, language arts, and social science, and give students a deeper understanding of how we learn about the past, as well as an appreciation for diversity among cultures.

What You Need

For the class:
- ❑ a few samples of natural objects gathered from the nearby environment
- ❑ a shopping bag, plastic or paper
- ❑ two yarn loops at least 15" in diameter
- ❑ a large class litter bag

For each group of four students:
- ❑ one shopping bag, plastic or paper
- ❑ two or three lengths of different colored yarn, to make loops at least 15" in diameter
- ❑ three index cards or sentence strips
- ❑ pencils
- ❑ newspaper or newsprint for covering tables

Getting Ready

1. Before class, take a walk around the nearby neighborhood of the school. Notice the types of natural and non-natural objects you see. Determine a route or an area that will allow each student to find several natural objects within about 15 minutes.

2. Gather five to ten samples of natural (leaves, sticks, seeds, rocks) and non-natural objects (bottle caps, candy wrappers, etc.) found in this area. Place these objects inside a large shopping bag. You will use these when introducing the activity to students.

Introducing Natural Objects

1. Gather the class and explain that they will be taking a short walk near the school. Ask the students to predict what NATURAL objects they might find; things that might have been there in the days of the Native Americans of 2,000 years ago. [rocks, plants, insects, etc.] Ask what objects they might find that are NOT natural. [cigarette butts, bottle caps, paper trash, plastics, etc.]

2. If students point out that an object could be both natural and not natural (a human-made object of wood or stone, for example), you might make a new category for those objects. Mention that ancient peoples used and modified natural objects for many different purposes (plant dyes, food, arrowheads, clothing, shelter, etc.).

3. Bring out the shopping bag with the objects you collected. Explain that you collected samples of objects you found on a walk. Place two yarn loops in front of you, so all students can see them.

4. Tell the students that natural objects go inside one yarn loop, and non-natural objects go in the other. As you show each object, ask if it is natural or not natural. Encourage students to explain why they chose a particular category. Have the students help you place the object inside the appropriate yarn loop. Objects that are both natural and not natural could be placed where both loops overlap.

If the environment around the school is not appropriate for collecting natural objects, you may decide to omit the walk and instead have students bring in natural objects from their own neighborhoods.

A student may ask about or you may want to note the distinction between indigenous plants that are native to the region and may well have been there 2000 years ago, and non-native plants that have been imported more recently.

Introducing the Walk

1. After having a student reiterate the difference between natural and not natural objects, discuss the following guidelines for the walk:

> • Students may collect natural objects only; they may collect only non-living objects.

> • Students may gather objects from the ground only; it is not okay to pick something that is growing on a plant, or in someone's garden!

> • If possible, students should gather multiples of an object (e.g. several oak leaves), and also collect as many different types of objects as possible.

2. When your students understand what kinds of objects to gather, divide them into groups of four and explain how they will work in their groups on the walk:

> • Each group of four students will collect their objects in one bag.

> • Whatever is put into the bag will be shared later by the group of four.

> • Groups may collect until their bag is about 1/3 to 1/2 full. (Show this amount with a sample bag)

> • Groups will have about 15 minutes, an assigned area in which to collect, and a signal to let them know when collecting time is finished.

> • Students may also collect non-natural litter and trash and put it into the class litter bag that you will carry. (Depending on the setting, you may want to caution students not to pick up broken glass, animal droppings, or other items that may pose health or safety hazards.)

3. Distribute a bag to each group of students, and escort students on the walk. At the designated time, return to the classroom.

This discussion could prompt an interesting opportunity to discuss the way different cultures and belief systems view the distinction between living and non-living entities. For example, in Native American and many other world cultures there are living spirits in the rocks and other natural objects and phenomena, and a great appreciation for the way that animals, plants, people, and the Earth are all part of one interacting and intertwined system.

Just before taking the walk, or during it, you may want to enrich students understanding of the idea of reciprocity that is so central to Native American cultures. The students are taking some objects from the natural environment for their use. In Native American practice, whether it be in planting and harvesting, hunting or obtaining materials for use in spiritual events, houses, tools, etc. this would always be accompanied by ceremonies and other ways to thank the natural world and take time to acknowledge what is being provided. Perhaps you and your students can come up with a small ritual to represent your appreciation, or can view the collection of litter as a positive contribution, a way of giving back to Mother Earth.

Free Exploration of the Collections

1. Gather the whole class together. Ask the students to describe briefly a few things that they found on the walk. What natural objects did they collect? What non-natural objects did they see? What else did they discover? Did anything surprise them?

2. Have each group of students place a piece of newspaper or newsprint on the center of their table, carefully empty the contents of their bag onto the paper, and freely explore the natural objects.

3. **Allow ample time for free exploration.** This is not only essential for students, it is valuable for you. As you circulate among the groups, you will have a chance to view the different ways students make sense of their collections. What kinds of observations are your students making? How are they organizing their objects? What types of descriptive words are they using? This time will also provide you an opportunity to assess group dynamics and behavior.

Sorting the Collections

1. When you feel students have had enough time for free exploration, regain the attention of the entire class. Ask each group of students to sort their objects into two separate piles, or categories.

Older students could be given the challenge of an open-ended, rather than a 2-group sort. Some students have arranged objects along a spectrum, made overlapping groups, or conducted other types of more complicated sorts. Challenge students who have more advanced sorting and classification skills to keep creating new categories.

> • They may sort any way they wish, as long as all group members agree on the method. Make clear that there are many possible ways to sort, and there is no "right" or "wrong" way to sort.
>
> • Give each group two yarn loops, one for each category. Mention that they may wish to create a third category, "outside the loops," for objects that do not fit into either loop.

2. As students work at this task, circulate among the groups. You will discover that the process is just as important as the product in this activity. You will have an opportunity to hear much discussion, and to see how students make observations, inferences, and decisions. You will also notice that groups have different methods and rates of proceeding. Allow enough time for each group to do at least one sort. If some groups have time, suggest that they do more than one sort.

3. Get the attention of the whole class, and have each group report about how they sorted their objects. On the chalkboard, create an ongoing list of categories students discovered. For example, one entry in the list might be "green/not green." This list may help to encourage students to create even more categories. In addition, the vocabulary words generated by students may become part of a glossary for subsequent writing activities.

4. If time permits, you may want to challenge groups of students to sort a second or third time, each time in a different way.

"Secret Sort"

1. Tell the students that you want to explain to them how to play a game called "Secret Sort." This time, each group will sort their objects into two piles as before, but they will not report how they sorted. Instead, for each pile, they will QUIETLY think of a word that describes the category, write the word on an index card, and place the card, face down, near the pile. For example, if they sorted into green/not green, they would write "green" on one card, "not green" on another card, and place each card, face down, near the appropriate pile. Demonstrate this procedure.

2. Distribute index cards and pencils, and have each group make a Secret Sort.

3. After all the groups have labeled their sorts, regain the attention of the entire class. Tell them that each group is going to have a chance to guess the Secret Sort of another group. Instruct each group to move, as a group, to another table (e.g., clockwise to the next table) and to work together to guess how the objects were sorted. When the group agrees, they may check their guess by turning over the labels.

4. If time permits, have each group rotate again to the next table. You may want to facilitate this rotation by using a signal, such as ringing a bell or flicking the lights. Before groups move, remind them to turn over the cards so they are face down for the next group.

5. When you feel it is appropriate, have students return to their original tables.

6. Ask students to report on the new categories they created or found. Add these to the list on the board. Ask students if they can think of additional possible ways to sort. Add these to the list.

7. If students are not going on to Session 3 immediately, have them put the objects back into their bags, label the bags with their names, and clean up their tables.

Evaluating Evidence

1. Conclude this session by asking students what they might be able to say about the neighborhood, based on what they have collected.

2. As you accept their responses, encourage the students to distinguish between their *observations* (based on direct *evidence*) and their *inferences* (what they conclude about what they've observed). For instance, if students found candy wrappers, that is direct evidence, and the presence of the wrappers is one of their observations. An inference from that observation might be that some people who live in or near the neighborhood eat candy. Similarly, from an observation of dry leaves, they might infer that it hasn't rained lately. These are possible, even likely inferences, but there are also other possible explanations.

3. Introduce the idea that the objects they found and the direct observations they made are like "clues" that can be used to make "intelligent guesses" to help explain more about the neighborhood.

Throughout this unit, you are asked to help students make "inferences," that is, to derive possible conclusions or explanations based on evidence and reasoning. Although the process of making at least simple inferences is appropriate for students of all ages, it is not at all necessary or advisable to use the word "inference" itself, especially not with younger students. You will probably want to use a more common word, such as "explanation" or "educated guess." Or you can talk about looking for "clues" to help find out more. For more on evidence and inference, see the "Background for Teachers" section of this guide.

You should also feel free to adapt or omit longer words like "anthropologist" or "mythology," etc., depending on your students' age and experience. The activities and the thinking processes they promote are the message here, not the vocabulary.

Session 1:   I liked this session the most because we got to collect neat things. What I liked most was when My friends Chris Corey Tait and I got a bees nest that was inside a hollow log. We also got to bring pieces of it home. My group also found other neat things like Fungi and really neat bark.

Session 2: Was my favorite session because we got to make a mask using your imaganation. And it was fun.

Session 1:
Krista Jeloniowski
I liked session 1: because, we to go out side and it was kind of like a scavenger hunt.

Session 2: Making Masks and Inferences

Overview

n the past, and in the present, people of all cultures have used masks for a variety of reasons. Native Americans from the Yosemite tribe in California and many other peoples have used masks to disguise themselves as animals when they went hunting. Natives of Kenya in Africa have used masks in helping cure people of disease. The Takun Indians of South America have a special mask for a girl to wear in a ceremony which celebrates her becoming a woman. The Hopi and Zuni tribes from the southwestern United States have Rain Masks to wear during celebrations to encourage rain spirits. Among the Iroquois people, Husk Face Masks are used to promote the growing of crops and in healing ceremonies. In some cultures, certain masks are extremely sacred objects that play an important part in spiritual and healing ceremonies, and as such are not to be viewed by others. The "Masks Resource Pages" on page 22 and 23 offer a glimpse of a few Native American and world masks.

The masks all peoples make reflect the materials available to the people at the time. Today, scientists study these fascinating art objects to learn more about the cultures, values and technologies of earlier and current civilizations.

In this session, your students use the objects they gathered in Session 1 to create their own masks. They observe patterns among the masks and make inferences about them. They use the masks in a variety of activities, including sorting and classification, writing, and dramatic arts.

What You Need

One teacher especially recommended "Tacky" glue for holding the natural materials onto the mask surface. This is an all-purpose glue available in hobby and crafts stores.

For each group of 4 students:
- ❑ 4 cardboard or card stock squares (approximately 8" by 8") or 4 paper plates (8" in diameter)
- ❑ 4 bottles of white glue (4 oz. size)
- ❑ 4 pairs of scissors
- ❑ bag of objects from Session 3
- ❑ newspaper for covering tables
- ❑ pencils

For the class:
- ❑ adhesive note paper ("post-its") or scrap paper (optional)

Getting Ready

You may want to consider having students work in groups to make a single mask. This can give students more experience working together on a very involving activity, and demonstrates how creativity can be enhanced and refined by cooperation and a group mix of ideas and skills.

1. Gather the newspaper, card stock, glue, scissors and bags of objects students collected, and have them ready to distribute after you have finished your introduction.

2. It is likely that some students will finish this activity before others. You could have books on masks available for early finishers, assign a "Going Further" activity, or adapt the "mask-family" idea noted on page 17.

Introducing the Masks

1. Explain to the students that many tribes and nations of Native Americans, as well as other peoples, have used all kinds of objects found in their environment to make masks. Elicit your students' ideas as to what purposes the masks might have served [rain ceremonies, celebrations, healing, harvests, dramatic performances, other special occasions].

2. Tell the students that they will each make their own mask with objects from their group's collection and that later on they will be using their masks in special ways.

3. Show them a sample piece of cardboard or paper plate that will become the base for the mask. The collected objects will be glued onto the base and will become features and decorations on the mask, such as eyes, noses, hair or earrings.

4. Encourage students be as creative as possible. They may want to imagine they are living in a different time and place, such as 2000 years ago, and make a mask accordingly. They may use the materials in any way they want. They may cut the base to reshape it. Students may choose to make masks with or without holes for the eyes.

5. Tell students that their first task will be to cover their work areas with newspaper. Next, have them put their names on the backs of their own masks.

6. Remind students that each group will share the materials the group collected. Establish rules for sharing by taking suggestions from students. These might include:

> • each group should find a fair way of dividing and sharing materials.
>
> • objects may be traded with other groups, as long as the process is quiet, and all group members agree.

7. Establish a time limit for the completion of the masks.

8. Distribute cardboard, glue, scissors, pencils and each group's collected objects. Remind students to write their names on the backs of the cardboard. Have students begin making their masks.

Making the Masks

1. While students are working on their masks, circulate among the groups. Help "stretch" students' creativity by asking them to tell you about their masks. You may want to pose questions such as:

- Does your mask have a name?

- Why did you choose the objects you used?

- What could your mask be used for?

2. As is true in most creative endeavors, students will proceed at varying rates. Try to allow ample time for all students to complete their maskmaking. Plan to have related activities available for the students who finish early. For example, you might direct an early finisher to create a name for her mask, and write a story about why it has its particular attributes. Or, you might have books about masks on hand for students to read during this time.

3. Of course, your schedule may necessitate ending the activity before all students have finished. In some classrooms, unfinished masks are put in a central area, and students are given the opportunity to complete them during recess or other free time.

4. When masks have been completed, have students clean up their work areas. Unused natural objects may be saved for future activities. Have students place their masks in a central display area to dry.

Sharing, Sorting, and Guessing Masks

1. Convene the students around the mask display area. Have them look carefully at the masks. (You may want to place a "post-it" or small sign, with a number, below each mask, for identification purposes.)

2. Ask for observations about the masks. For example, are there any masks that are similar? How are they alike? What

One teacher asked students who finished early to draw the faces of the "family" members of the main mask they made. Students were very enthusiastic, and planned their families according to various common characteristics, sometimes giving "special powers" to them. They wrote down what powers each family member had (could bring rain, fertility, etc.) If any of your students do this, they could also use other members of their mask's family to help them dramatize the myths they create and share in the next two sessions.

are some differences between masks? Challenge students to sort or "graph" the masks by attributes: for example, happy/not happy; hair/no hair, etc. Encourage students to make up their own categories for sorting the masks. The possibilities are endless.

3. Conduct a mask guessing game. Without telling the students which mask you are referring to, describe it, being as specific as possible. Challenge the students to identify which mask you have described. They may refer to the masks by number. Continue to provide additional details, as needed, until the students guess which mask you are describing.

4. Ask for volunteers to describe masks while other students guess.

Making Inferences Based on Masks

1. Remind the students of their discussion about the neighborhood of their walk, based on what they observed and the objects they collected. They made guesses, or inferences, based on the evidence they saw and collected.

2. Explain that this is the same process that *anthropologists* must use when studying objects they have found, including masks that come from ancient cultures. Anthropologists study much more than masks; their research includes learning about people and their cultures, both past and present, all over the world. Anthropologists cannot experience ancient peoples or events directly, but they can study masks and other objects, as well as any stories and legends that have been passed on, to learn more about the people who created them.

3. Tell the students to imagine that their mask creations are a collection of masks in a museum. Ask the students to act as anthropologists as they look at each mask. Ask:

  • What might the mask have been used for?

  • What can you tell about the people who made the mask and about their environment?

  • What about the mask makes you think that?

4. Lead a discussion that focuses on an appreciation of distinctiveness and *diversity*. Ask questions such as:

  • What similarities and differences did you notice between masks?

• Why might masks made in different times or places be different?

• Do you think it's important to find out about different ways of doing things? Why?

• What additional discoveries did you make?

5. Provide a designated area of the classroom for a "museum" display or storage of the masks for possible use later in the unit.

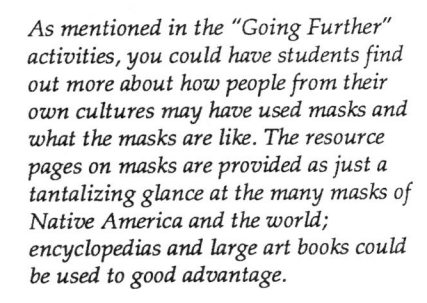

As mentioned in the "Going Further" activities, you could have students find out more about how people from their own cultures may have used masks and what the masks are like. The resource pages on masks are provided as just a tantalizing glance at the many masks of Native America and the world; encyclopedias and large art books could be used to good advantage.

Going Further for Sessions 1 & 2

1. Ask students to collect natural objects found in their own neighborhoods, or on their block, with safety cautions as needed. Invite them to bring the objects to share and to compare with each other.

2. Provide additional time, in class or at home, for students to write or dictate descriptions or stories about their masks. The written descriptions could become part of a permanent display with the masks.

3. Have students mount the masks on popsicle sticks or tongue depressors and use them for dramatic play.

4. Ask small groups of students to create "families" of masks. Have the students collaborate to write a story or perform a play about their group's mask family. See the note on page 17 for a little more on mask families.

5. Have a parade around the school with the masks, so that other classrooms may view the fruits of the students' labor. One school in Spokane Washington used the masks to create a totem pole for their school.

6. If there ia a Native American artist who specializes in making masks in your locale, arrange for her to visit the classroom or the class to visit her workshop.

7. Ask students to bring in pictures of masks from magazines or real masks from home. Have them speculate about the purposes of the masks. Use these masks as a springboard for encouraging students to conduct further investigations about the cultures from which the masks originated.

8. Encourage students to find out how their ancestors used masks or how today's cultures use masks.

9. Put on display around the room, pictures, posters, and books showing a variety of masks from different cultures. Direct each student to select a mask to study. They might make a list of the materials they can identify in the mask. They might describe the information they can infer from the mask. They might also sketch how the mask may have been used by the culture. These reports can be used as an assessment of how each student applies what he/she has learned from participating in these activities.

One class in the Pacific Northwest made their masks out of paper bags then piled them on top of each other to create a totem pole effect. This could also be done by fastening the paper plate masks in vertical fashion on a wall.

TOTEM POLE

Native American MASKS
Resource Page

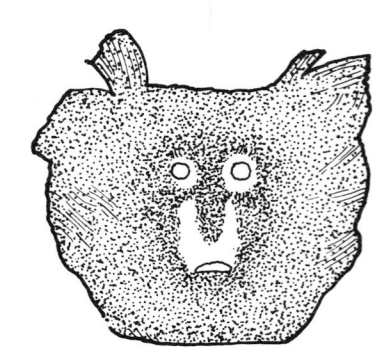

An artist's interpretation of an Iroquois cornhusk mask, or Husk Face. A great variety of these intricately braided, coiled, and or twined masks are used in many important ceremonies. They are said to represent a class of spirits who originally joined with human beings to teach hunting and agriculture; their dramatic appearance at the Midwinter Festival symbolizes the gift of maize, beans, and squash. They are very important in healing and purification, and their use is accompanied by songs, dances, and many other ceremonies. The other main kind of masks made by the Iroquois are the striking "False Face" masks, made of wood and other materials. The sacred nature of many of these masks has led to demands that those in museums and private collections be returned to the Iroquois societies that originated them, and to controversy about the unsuitability of public exhibition.

Drawing of a Thunderbird Mask of the Kwakiutl people of the Northwest Coast of North America. The mask is shown open, as the bird's beaks and wings open to reveal a human face. The face is interpreted as symbolizing the inner spirit, or inua, and thus combines the human and the spiritual entity represented by the the bird or animal mask. In the dramatization of one myth, for example, the wearer opens the beak when the Thunderbird spirit succeeds in showing a man how to build a house. The mask is made of painted wood and its full width is 1.82 meters. Other materials used in intricate Kwakiutl masks include: abalone, animal teeth and bird beaks, bark, fur, leather hinges, hammered copper.

An artist's interpretation of a woodchuck fur mask of the Cherokee people. Many masks were originally used for hunting or for ceremonies or stories connected to animals and their spirits. Some Cherokee stories begin with phrases like, "This is what the old people told me, when I was a child, about the days when people and animals could still speak to one another…" (See the reference listings for an audiotape of animal stories told by Gayle Ross, the great-great-great granddaughter of John Ross, the Principal Chief of the Cherokee nation during the time of the Trail of Tears, when they were forced off their homeland in the Southeast by the U.S. government when gold was discovered, and many thousands died.)

Two Hopi Kachina masks, the Bear Kachina and the Deer Kachina. The Bear Kachina is said to have great strength in healing. A dancer with this mask appears in the Mixed Kachina dance, and many other dances and ceremonies. The Deer Kachina has power over the rain, and also represents a prayer for the increase of deer. These are but two of many Hopi masks used in healing and many other ceremonies, dances, prayers, and blessings.

Selected World
MASKS
Resource Page

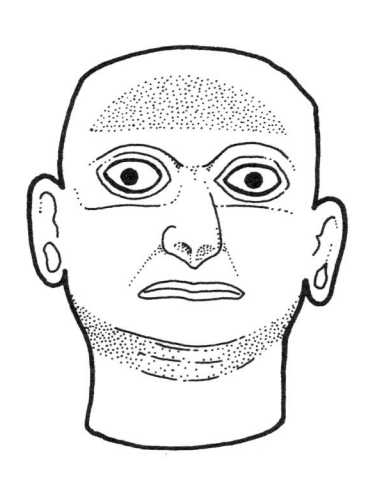

A mask used in Sri Lanka, one of 19 "disease devil" masks, used in healing ceremonies. This one is used to help cure deafness.

A death mask of the Incan royalty made of metal, with ears that move, from the Moon Pyramid in Peru.

A Javanese *tupeng* mask, made of wood, metal, cloth, and horsehair, representing the witch Rangda, used in theatrical presentations on Java and Bali.

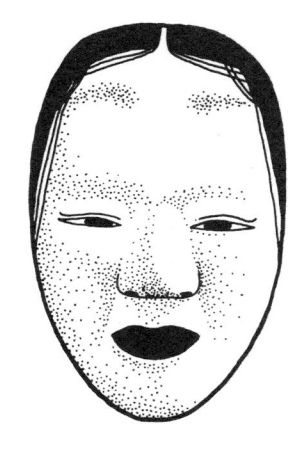

A Nō mask, typical of those worn in classical Japanese drama. There are about 125 varieties of these, carefully stylized and representing different characterizations.

A maiden spirit mask of painted wood from the Ibo Ekpe people of Africa.

All around the world masks are used in many different ways, from the sacred to the profane, the sublime to the ridiculous. You may want to have your students do group projects on the main uses and many kinds of masks. It is interesting to compare the ways that masks are used by different cultures. For example, in researching these brief pages, some interesting similarities were noted in the healing masks of the Iroquois and those of the Sinhalese people of Sri Lanka.

You have noticed

that everything an Indian does is in a circle, and that is

because the Power of the World always works in circles, and everything

tries to be round. In the old days when we were a strong and happy people, all our

power came to us from the sacred hoop of the nation, and so long as the hoop was

unbroken, the people flourished. The flowering tree was the living center of the hoop, and the

circle of the four quarters nourished it. The east gave peace and light, the south gave warmth, the west

gave rain, and the north with its cold and mighty wind gave strength and endurance. This knowledge

came to us from the outer world with our religion. Everything the Power of the World does is done in

a circle. The sky is round, and I have heard that the earth is round like a ball, and so are all the stars.

The wind, in its greatest power, whirls. Birds make their nests in circles, for theirs is the same

religion as ours. The sun comes forth and goes down again in a circle. The moon does the

same, and both are round. Even the seasons form a great circle in their changing and

always come back again to where they were. The life of a man is a circle

from childhood to childhood, and so it is in everything

where   power   moves.   ●

Reprinted with permission from *Black Elk Speaks: Being the Life Story of a Holy Man of the Oglala Sioux*, as told through John G. Neihardt (Flaming Rainbow), with an introduction by Vine Deloria, Jr. University of Nebraska Press, Lincoln and London, paperback edition, 1988. From the beginning of Chapter XVII, "The First Cure."

Session 3: Creating Myths

Overview

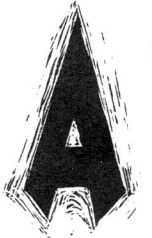

A myth is a story or legend that is passed on by a people over many generations. Myths can help explain or comment upon the relationship between a people and the world around them. Like masks, myths have a special role in many Native American and world cultures. Some myths are sacred and are to be told only by certain people at certain times. These are a part of a system of belief and are an important part in the spiritual life and practice of the specific tribe or nation involved. Other stories are told over and over by all kinds of people. These stories often teach important lessons. In this activity, we focus on myths or stories that also explain or in some way represent or symbolize the natural world.

For more information on the use of the word myth, and the role of "stories" in Native American cultures, please see the "Background for Teachers" section. The reference listing contains two books by Michael Caduto and Joseph Bruchac that provide outstanding background on stories and storytelling in tribal culture.

In this session, your students imagine themselves living where they do now, only it's 2000 years ago. After a discussion of what would not be found long ago, your students focus on things Native peoples of those days might have observed that are present today, such as mountains, water, animals, plants and the sky. Your students hear brief summaries of two Native American stories, as examples of how stories can explain natural phenomena.

Your students are then challenged to create stories of their own to explain one of the following: why there is night and day, why the moon changes its shape, how the stars came to be, a storm ending with a rainbow, and a caterpillar changing into a butterfly. Each team of two students creates a story and draws pictures of events in their stories. (Writing down the stories is optional.)

You may want to read a number of Native American myths out loud in the weeks before this unit or before you begin this activity. This may help students see how a story can help explain or symbolically represent a natural phenomenon. As with the masks activity, **free expression and full creativity are to be greatly encouraged.**

The stories and oral narratives of Native peoples throughout the Americas, from the Inuit to the Inca, are part of interwoven, distinctive, and complex systems of belief. The stories are but excerpts of much more extensive narratives and complete, sufficient cultures. The teacher's guide for Keepers of the Earth (the outstanding collection of stories and activities by Michael J. Caduto and Joseph Bruchac) says it best, "Stories are at the very center of the lives of the Native peoples of North America. Whether they are used as a means of instruction or as a vital ingredient in a healing ceremony, stories serve the people in many ways. Stories offer insight into how Native North Americans seek to explain the seemingly inexplicable in creation, cosmology, and natural science—to answer the age-old question of 'why?' These tales also help Native peoples see more clearly the true value of their environments and the best ways to maintain a healthy balance with nature. Perhaps, if we listen closely, these stories may do the same."

One kindergarten teacher had a class of second graders come into her class to share their myths with the younger students. This is a great idea! The older students loved sharing their stories, and by doing so, they modelled the task in a way that helped the younger students create their own myths. If you can work with other teachers in this way, we highly recommend it.

What You Need

For the Class:

❏ The 5 full-page pictures of the stars, moon, sun, rainbow, and butterfly, provided at the end of this guide (or any additional pictures you may wish to use, see "Getting Ready.")

❏ 1 to 5 pieces colored construction paper (11" x 19") to use as backing for the full-page pictures

❏ 1 wide-tipped felt marking pen to write captions (optional)

❏ 1 roll masking tape

❏ chalkboard or large paper to record ideas

For Each Pair of Students:

❏ 1 or 2 sheets of large drawing or newsprint paper, 19" x 11" (large construction paper size)

❏ 1 sheet of lined writing paper (optional)

❏ 2 pencils

❏ 1 set of crayons or colored felt pens

Getting Ready

1. There are five pictures (the moon, sun, stars, a rainbow and a butterfly) of natural phenomena in the back of the guide. Decide which of them you wish to display for the activity. If you wish, have a student color the pictures, especially the rainbow and the butterfly. Depending on the age of your students, use one or more of the pictures. For better focus, we suggest limiting the total number of pictures you display to five. If you have other large pictures you prefer to use, either of the same phenomena or different ones (a volcano or a parrot, for instance) feel free to include them instead of the ones provided.

S U N

M O O N

S T A R S

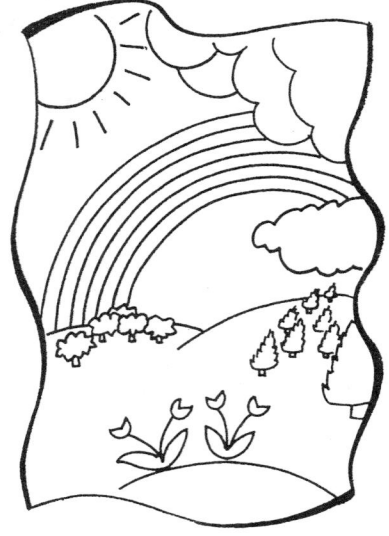

R A I N B O W

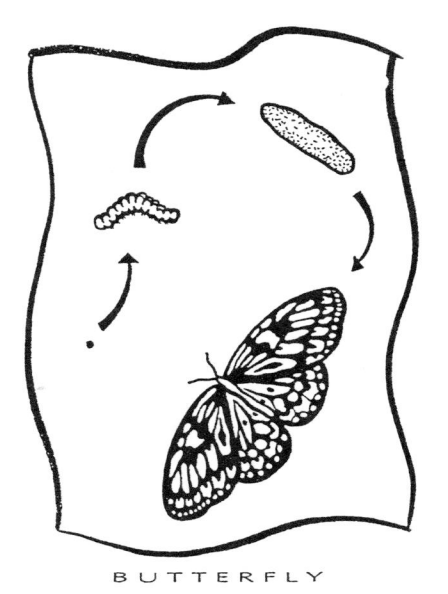

B U T T E R F L Y

2. We suggest mounting the pictures on large construction paper for display. We have provided sample captions below. You may wish to write these on the construction paper below the pictures, especially for older students. Whether you choose to write the captions or just read them aloud to the students, the verbal descriptions may help students focus on the phenomena that they will be attempting to explain with their myths.

You may want to put these pictures up before beginning the session, so students see them around the room, or you can put them up during the class, as the text suggests.

Suggested Captions for the Pictures

Sun
A very hot, bright light goes across the sky every day.

Moon
A shape of light appears in the sky. It changes slowly from a thin shape to a round shape, then slowly gets thinner again.

Stars
When it is dark and there are no clouds, we see many small, bright lights in the sky.

There are many other observations of the natural world you might choose to highlight in place of those suggested. Volcanoes, lightning, earthquakes, "shooting stars" or more predictable events, especially seasonal change, have also inspired many stories and myths. Resist the temptation to present a long list, however. Your students may focus more successfully if you have them choose from a short "menu" of a few natural observations.

Butterfly
A caterpillar changes to a chrysalis and then to a butterfly.

Rainbow
Dark clouds gather, a heavy rain falls, then the sun comes out and a rainbow arches across the sky.

3. Decide if you wish to let the students use their masks for inspiration in Session 3 and/or as a part of their sharing of myths in Session 4. If you plan to include the masks, have them handy.

4. Decide how you want to form pairs of students for the activity. Some teachers find it valuable to assign partners carefully ahead of time. Others pair students at random or let students choose their own partners. If you feel that your students, especially in kindergarten or first grade, will do better working individually on their myths and drawings, adjust accordingly.

Setting the Stage

What People Observed Long Ago

1. Ask the class to imagine that they are living right where they are now, except that it's 2000 years ago. Depending on your students' sense of history, help them understand how long ago that was. Were there any people here besides many tribes and nations of Native Americans? [No, not till much later.] Were there dinosaurs 2000 years ago? [No, dinosaurs lived much longer ago than that. They did not live at the same time as humans.] Were there cars? Airplanes? Ask your students to think of other things that were not here 2000 years ago. [TVs, bikes, telephones, plastic objects, clocks, etc.]

2. Have the class list some of the things that they would have seen around them 2000 years ago. Record their answers on the chalkboard. To elicit a variety of ideas, you might ask, "What might we see on the ground? In the water? In the sky?" Record all their ideas. If there is disagreement about whether an animal or object existed in your area 2000 years ago, take a little time to discuss it, or just put a question mark after it on the list.

Introducing Myths

1. Explain that Native Americans of long ago were very careful observers of the world around them. Like all peoples in all times, they told stories. Some of the stories were told over and over for many years, and, as they were passed on, came to be, and in many cases still are, a very important part of people's lives and beliefs. Explain that one word for special stories like these is *"myths."* You may want to write the word on the board.

2. Different tribes and nations have different ways of life and different myths or stories. Some stories are serious and important, and can be told only by certain people on special occasions. Others are funny or have a lesson to teach. Such stories often explain or reflect things that people saw and wondered about.

Two Examples

1. As an example, tell the class the Modoc people, who lived near a volcano now called Mount Shasta in California, often saw smoke coming out of the top of the mountain. They told a story in which the mountain was a giant lodge or teepee for the sky gods or spirits. The smoke coming out the top was from the gods' cooking fire. This is not only an interesting

You may want to point out that peoples of long ago probably paid much more attention to the events of nature than most people do today, because then they didn't have things like TV, or cars, or asphalt and cement paving over the earth. People spent more time outside than most of us do and observed nature carefully. Agricultural work, the domestication and hunting of animals, and numerous other economic and cultural activities intertwined with nature. Their physical survival and beliefs about life were very related to the cycles of night and day and the seasons. They observed the movements of the stars and planets to know when to plant and harvest crops and felt a very close spiritual kinship with animals and plants. Different tribes and nations had many different ways of life, beliefs, and stories, but all were very connected to the natural world in one way or another.

The two stories summarized in extremely brief form here are adapted from Stories California Indians Told by Anne B. Fisher and California Indian Nights by Edward Gifford and Gwendoline Harris Block.

story, it helps explain or illustrate something in nature. (If you have read other stories to the class, you may want to ask students to give similar examples from them.)

2. As an example of how a story might explain the origin of the Sun and Moon, you can briefly summarize a story told by the Pomo people of California. Explain that tule (pronounced too-lee) grass is a tall marsh grass that grows in what is now Northeastern California. In the story, Coyote makes a huge ball of tule grass and gives it and some flint rocks to Hawk. Hawk flies high in the sky, lights the ball of grass on fire with a spark from the flint, and thus creates the Sun. Coyote then makes the Moon from a ball of damp tule grass, so when Hawk sets it on fire it burns less brightly. Sometimes the moon is only partly lighted because the wind blows part of its fire out.

If your feel your students would benefit from modelling the process of generating a story, you might spend five or ten minutes making up an example together, as a class. As the students add ideas, you or one of the students could draw a picture that illustrates the sample myth.

3. If you think your students need more examples of ways that stories can explain or model the workings of natural phenomena, use a few of the stories outlined on pages 39 and 40. You might choose to read some of them aloud, or copy the pages for students to read. Remember, the object here is to convey the idea of making up a story that explains natural phenomena, not duplicating the Native American or world stories. If you do not feel that your students need these examples before creating their own stories, save the myths on these pages to share after the students have shared their own myths in Session 4.

4. Put up the five pictures of natural phenomena that you have chosen to use, and mention that these are all things that Native Americans could observe in nature long ago that we still observe today.

Explaining Observations Through Myths

1. Ask your students to pretend that they are living 2000 years ago. Like people from that time, they are very close observers of nature.

2. Explain that they will work with a partner to create a story together. Like the Native American stories they've heard about, their stories should explain how something came to be the way it is.

3. Encourage creativity by telling them that their stories can have animals or people with super powers. They can use their imaginations to make up a funny or serious or action-packed story.

4. Tell them that each team of partners should first choose one of the pictures to explain with a story. Take a moment to let students get settled in their work spaces with their partners to discuss which picture to choose. Have teams write "Stars," "Moon," "Rainbow," etc. on their papers to indicate which natural phenomena they have chosen.

5. Make it clear that the goal is for partners to make up a story **together**, along with a drawing showing what happens in their story. Later, they will be able to share their story and drawing with the class. Tell them that they can wear the masks they made when they tell their story, or use the masks in other dramatic ways.

6. It is not necessary for students to write down their stories. Teams can simply discuss their story and make a drawing. However, depending on your students' ages and abilities, some teams may wish to compose their story in writing on paper first, then make a drawing that shows what happens in their story. In a class with a large spectrum of abilities, you might give the students the option to write, but require only the drawing.

7. Suggest that the students begin drawing in pencil so they can erase if necessary, and later color their pictures with crayons or pens. Explain that they should draw BIG pictures so other people will be able to see them from far away when they share with the class. Emphasize that their pictures can be in whatever style they prefer. On the chalkboard, draw a stick-figure coyote or person to show that a picture can communicate well without being fancy or perfect.

8. If your students have not had much experience collaborating in small groups, talk for a few minutes about how to share the task. If one partner likes to draw, the other could do more of the coloring, or could label the parts of the picture and write the title. They should both write their names on the back of their paper. Stories should include ideas from both partners.

9. Focus the class on the challenge of attempting to describe and explain the natural phenomena with a story. After making sure that the students understand their task, distribute paper, pencils and crayons or markers, and have them begin.

The Activity: Students Create Myths

1. As students work, circulate, giving encouragement. If a team is having trouble getting started, you might suggest a "story-starting" sentence such as, "Once, there were no stars..." You could also help spur ideas by asking questions like, "What do the stars remind you of?" "What animal would you like to have in your story?" "How could that animal help make the stars?" Encourage imaginative and creative storytelling.

2. For some students, knowledge of modern, scientific explanations may make the storytelling task confusing. You may want to note to these students that many different peoples developed accurate scientific and mathematical knowledge thousands of years ago, but they also passed on beliefs and visualized what they wondered about in nature through stories and myths. Emphasize to these students that the idea here is to put themselves back to a time 2000 years ago, to think carefully about what they would actually observe about the natural phenomena they have chosen, then use their creative imaginations to make up a story to help explain what is taking place.

3. With some groups, you may want to remind them of the task by asking them to ask themselves if their story helps explain how or why something happens; how or why a caterpillar becomes a butterfly—how or why the moon has different shapes.

4. Remind students to draw large pictures, and label them if possible. Students who want a greater challenge could make stories that explain more than one of the phenomena. They could also plan how to use their masks when they dramatize the stories in the next session. When most students have finished, collect their drawings and written stories, if they wrote them down. These will be shared in the next session.

*Of course, your students have only a short time in class to do this. You may want to note that this is very different than the long time over which traditional myths develop to become a treasured, respected, and often sacred part of a people's heritage, being told over and over again for perhaps thousands of years. But maybe some of the myths and legends we know today started long ago with a simple story that began with wondering and imagination. **Maybe some began with two people sitting around a campfire looking at the stars.***

You may also want to refer students having difficulty to the list the class generated during the earlier discussion of "What People Observed Long Ago," suggesting that one of the animals or other things listed might become a character or part in their story.

With older students you may also want to discuss the fact that today, as in the past, people related and wrote not only fictional stories, but also non-fiction of many different types.

Turtle Island Mother Earth

To begin with there was no earth, only water,
With animals who swam or flew nearby–
Then there came a wondrous human Daughter
Who fell down from a torn place in the sky.
She needed soil of earth, or she would die.

Two Loons cried out and caught her as she fell,
Called for the other animals to lend a paw,
Set her to rest upon a giant Turtle's shell,
Began to dive into the Sea's vast craw,
To seek the earthly soil with tooth and claw.

The Beaver tried, his broad tail slapped the tide,
A Muskrat lent his whiskers to the search,
When they came up the Turtle looked inside
Their mouths to see if they had captured any earth.
Others tried and failed, returned to their sad perch.

Poor Toad stayed down so long he almost died,
But in his mouth, so deep the Toad had dived,
Turtle found a mound of earth (Toad glowed inside)
The wondrous Daughter of the sky survived!
She patted earth around the Turtle's shell, revived!

The soil began to grow and grow, becoming land,
Earth grew and grew upon Great Turtle's shell,
From clumps and countries continents expand.
Then Woman brought forth Children, with their Truths to tell,
Maize, beans, and pumpkins sprout from Her as well.

So Children of today, please listen as we say
That this Daughter from the sky created our Life's way
And were it not for the animals, like the Loons and the Toad,
Who knows what might have happened on Life's long road?
It's still a question, a mystery—if not for that Turtle, where would we be?

Session 4: Sharing Myths

Overview

f we listen with respect and appreciation, myths can teach us much us about a people, past or present. In thinking about what can be learned about a culture from its myths, your students discover that myths contain much more than just explanations and stories about observations of the natural world. Myths also record the ways and beliefs of a people, and help sustain their culture. Learning more about a people's mythology, or studying their myths, is one of the ways that anthropologists search for clues to the past.

In this session, your students share the myths they created in Session 3. Some may want to use the masks they made to assist them in dramatizing their myths. Take time to appreciate each story and presentation, and to encourage respectful listening and understanding.

After hearing "How the Stars Came to Be," (and/or any other stories you prefer) your students are asked what they can infer about the people who told the story(ies). Your students are also asked to consider what a future anthropologist might infer about them from their stories.

One teacher led her class in a guided visualization, having them close their eyes, take some deep breaths, think peaceful thoughts, and imagine themselves sitting around a campfire long ago. She encouraged a feeling of connection to the plants and animals, and asked the students to visualize the natural world around them, from the mountains in the distance to the rush of the nearby stream. Then she began the sharing of the stories, having set a special mood. Doing this also conveys a certain reverence and respect for stories and storytelling that is consistent with the special times for telling, ceremonial settings, and great respect they receive within Native American cultures. It also encourages the patience, listening skills, not interrupting others, and general respectfulness for others that are all part of the traditional ways that these stories are passed on and learned by new generations.

What You Need

❑ the pictures (sun, moon, rainbow, etc.) from the previous session
❑ student drawings (and written stories, if any) from the previous session
❑ 1 roll of masking tape

Getting Ready

1. Choose a wall on which to display the students' drawings so they can be seen by the whole class.

2. Is possible, arrange the drawings in groups, near the pictures of the natural phenomena they seek to explain.

3. Have the student masks available for their use in dramatizing their stories.

Sharing the Students' Stories

Among the Iroquois and a number of other peoples around the world, notably in Africa, the highly-respected and gifted people who became storytellers had a "storyteller's bag," filled with items, such as a cornhusk doll, that acted as mnemonic devices. In their Keepers of the Earth teacher's guide, Caduto and Bruchac note: "Making a storyteller's bag is a project that can be adopted by a teacher. You and your students can gather items from the natural world or make things to add to the bag. Feathers, stones, small carvings, animal teeth, anything that can be jostled around in a bag without breaking can be part of your collection." For this GEMS activity, you could even make a class storyteller's bag for the Session 4 story sharing, and decide the order in which teams tell their stories by reaching into the class bag to pick a small object or drawing each team has contributed.

1. When the class has gathered, and can see the displayed drawings, tell them that you'd like them to imagine that it is nighttime long ago, and that they have gathered in the evening around the fire, just as Native Americans may have done. There's no radio or TV. There are wonderful stories to share.

2. Ask a team of volunteers to come up and stand near their drawing as they tell their story and describe what their picture shows. If students also want to use their masks, you might suggest that the mask be the image of the storyteller. Or, students could use the masks as characters in their story-drama.

3. Since some students may be shy about telling their stories to the class, you may not want to require everyone to share. On the other hand, if you have too many eager storytellers for one class period, you may want to save some of the stories for a different time.

4. When everyone has shared, tell them that they've done a wonderful job of explaining some things in the natural world through stories. For older students, remind them that explanations based on observations can be called inferences.

5. Point out that scientists try to explain their observations with inferences too. Ask if anyone knows what most of today's scientists think about stars. [They are gigantic balls of burning gases, and look small because they are so far away.] Say that scientists keep testing their inferences, and when they make new observations, they often have to change their inferences.

Sharing "How the Stars Came To Be"

1. Depending on the age level and backgrounds of your students, you should emphasize that, when we talk about Native Americans, this includes many diverse nations and tribes of distinct peoples. Native, or *Indigenous* peoples, live throughout North and South America, Central America and the Caribbean. These are peoples of the present as well as the original inhabitants of this part of the world.

2. Explain that passing on lessons and beliefs in oral traditions and special spiritual ceremonies has been and is important in all these cultures, but each culture also has its own special characteristics. (For younger students, having culturally sensitive books or video resources on different tribes available in the classroom introduces this diversity and can bring in the present-day realities as well.)

3. You may also want to stress that while Native American stories are wonderful and powerful, they are certainly not the only ways that Native Americans, or any other peoples with ancient roots, look at the world. Numerous scientific, agricultural, mathematical, social, and cultural accomplishments of Native American peoples have transformed and enriched the world — and continue to do so. There were many other kinds of scientific, mathematical, and technological ideas developed by people all over the world before our time, and our own ideas are constantly changing too.

Two excellent books by Jack Weatherford, an anthropologist, provide a good basis for learning more. One is entitled Indian Givers: How the Indians of the Americas Transformed the World, and the other is called Native Roots: How the Indians Enriched America. Full reference listings are in the adult reference section at the back of the book.

4. Tell the class that you'd like to share a story with them, and that they should listen carefully to see what the story might be able to tell us about the people who created it, and what its lessons are. Tell them that the story is called "How the Stars Came to Be." Read aloud the story on the next page.

HOW THE STARS CAME TO BE

Once, it was always daytime. All the animals enjoyed constant sunlight and warmth because there was no night. But the animals did not get along well with each other. They argued and fought so much that the Sky Spirits looked down and said, "The animals must learn to cooperate and be friends. We will teach them a lesson."

The Sky Spirits threw a blanket over the sky. Everything in the world was suddenly dark and cold. The animals were frightened and kept bumping into each other. Finally, Bear said, "Everyone gather in the big meadow so we can figure out what to do!"

When all the animals had found their way in the dark to the big meadow, Bear announced, "The sky is covered with a blanket. We need to get the light back! We need to get the blanket off the sky!" The bears decided to try making a bear pyramid to reach the sky. Many strong bears formed the bottom layer, and others climbed on their backs. But the third layer of bears was too heavy. The pyramid of bears fell down before it had come anywhere near the sky.

Then the snakes said, "We can reach the sky!" They began to slither together to make a tall tower. The tower reached higher than the pyramid of bears had, but soon it began to sway back and forth. Though the snakes tried very hard, their tower fell over before it could reach the sky.

Hummingbird called out, "Let me try!" All the animals said, "No! You're too small!" But she began to fly up, up, up. The animals heard her humming far above, and they began to cheer her on. "Fly, Hummingbird. You can do it!" Hummingbird reached the blanket that had been thrown over the sky and poked a hole in it with her tiny beak! A small, bright light shone through—a star! She made many more stars as the animals cheered and joined together to celebrate below.

As the light from the stars came to the meadow, the Sky Spirits looked down and saw the animals cheering for Hummingbird and being nice to each other. They said, "We will take the blanket off the sky now. But every night we will put it back, to remind the animals of the lesson they have learned."

Note: We learned this story from a Lawrence Hall of Science staff teacher. We have incomplete information on the specific origin of the story, and are continuing our research. If you can help us with any information about the source of this story, its tribal or cultural context, or different versions, please let us know.

Mythology: Finding Clues to the Past

1. Ask the class for any reactions to the story of "How the Stars Came to Be." Elicit student ideas or guesses (inferences) about the people who told the story. For example, ask, "What can we say about the life and beliefs of the people who told that story?" [They lived in an area where there were both bears and hummingbirds, they believed in "Sky Spirits," they seem to greatly value kindness and cooperation, they probably used blankets, etc.]

2. Encourage all responses and ask questions to assist students to explain the part of the story on which they based their inference. Can we be sure of our inferences, or just make a guess that they might be true? (For older students, emphasize that the story, its characters, plots, and events, constitutes *evidence* from which to derive *inferences* about the people who originated it. Like all stories, it also includes lessons and values.)

3. Explain that just as anthropologists study masks, they also study myths and make inferences about the people who told them. *Mythology*, the study of myths, helps anthropologists find clues to the past and is the source of much of the world's great literature.

4. If there is time, share another story or stories, perhaps one you have chosen that is told by the Native inhabitants of your region, or one you find particularly interesting for your students. After each story, ask the students for their inferences about the people who told it.

5. Focus the class on their own stories once again. Ask your students what a future anthropologist might infer about them by studying their myths. If time allows and students are interested, generate a list of inferences that someone might make from your students' stories.

It would be interesting to compare and contrast some of the Native American stories with the legends about Paul Bunyan, John Henry, Davy Crockett, and other "tall tales" that are in so many children's books. What are the attitudes toward the natural world that come through in the stories? What about the attitudes toward Native peoples in the stories about westward expansion?

Going Further (for Sessions 3 and 4)

1. Invite a Native American storyteller and/or anthropologist to the class to expand upon the role that storytelling and myth plays in the life of the people or peoples they are a part of and/or have studied.

2. Invite students to share a myth or legend that is from their culture, or that is an important part of their family history or folklore. Discuss what inferences can be drawn from these stories.

3. Collect together all the myths and legends the class has heard or read during the year. Have a special session to summarize and comment on them. You could discuss the various ways the stories reveal information about the people and cultures who created them, and look for common themes that unite them despite their differences in origin. This would be an excellent introduction or accompaniment to a curriculum focus on world literature.

NATIVE AMERICAN MYTHS RESOURCE PAGE

1. *Rainbow Crow* **from the Lenape people of what is now Pennsylvania, explains the crow's feathers and voice.**

Long ago, the Earth was always cold and snowy. Back then, Crow was the most colorful bird, with the sweetest voice. So the animals picked him to fly to the Great Sky Spirit to ask for warmth. Crow sang so sweetly to the Sky Spirit that he was given the warm gift of fire. But as he flew home with a flaming stick in his mouth, Crow's feathers turned black, and the smoke and ash made his voice cracked and hoarse. Still, for being so brave and unselfish, the Sky Spirit gave Crow the gift of rainbows shining in his black feathers, and told him, "the two-legged will never hunt you for your meat tastes like fire and smoke..."

2. *How Snake Brought Rain* **from the Shoshone people of Nevada and Wyoming, explains the rainbow.**

Once there was no rain. Snake offered to use his scaly skin to scrape ice loose from the clouds so that it would fall, be melted by the Sun, and become rain. The Shaman threw Snake high into the sky. Snake arched from the South to the North end of the sky, and began to scrape ice from the clouds. It rained until the thirst of the land and all living things was quenched. When the weather cleared, the people could see Snake in the sky, glowing with all the colors of the sky and world.

3. *A Story of the Sun and Moon* **from the Maidu people of Butte and Plumas counties in California: explains how Sun and Moon rose into the sky.**

Sun and Moon were sister and brother. But instead of rising and traveling over the world every day as the people wanted, they stayed in their house. Then Gopher and Angle Worm burrowed inside the house, carrying a bag of fleas. Once inside, Gopher opened the bag. Sun and Moon became so itchy and miserable they decided to leave the house. Sun traveled by day so all the stars wouldn't fall in love with her. Her brother Moon agreed to travel by night.

4. *The Moon's Phases* **from the Karok people of Humboldt County, California.**

Moon was disliked by everybody. Many people visited Moon and tried to get rid of him. Lizard managed to start eating Moon, but just as he was nearly finished, Frog Woman, one of Moon's wives, came and chased Lizard away. Since then, Lizard is always returning and eating Moon, and each time Frog Woman chases him away and makes Moon over again.

5. *Six Wives Who Ate Wild Onions* **from the Monache people of central California, explains how the constellation the Pleiades came to be.**

One day, while their husbands were hunting cougar, six young women found sweet wild onions to eat. When their husbands came home, they complained of the smell, saying the cougars would smell the onions and run away. The men sent their wives outside, but they couldn't sleep in the cold, and decided to leave their husbands. One wife brought her baby girl. Using magic ropes the wives rose up·in the sky and became a group of bright stars. The husbands were sorry they had sent their wives away, but the wives stayed in the sky. They are still there...

The myths/stories above were adapted and summarized from the following resources: (1) *Rainbow Crow* by Nancy Van Laan; (2) *Indian Masks and Myths* of the West by Joseph H. Wherry; (3) and (4)*California Indian Nights* by Edward W. Gifford and Gwendoline Harris Block; (5) *They Dance in the Sky, Native American Star Myths*, Jean Guard Monroe and Ray A. Williamson. See the Resources section for full reference listing.

WORLD CULTURES MYTHS RESOURCE PAGE

1. Ancient Egyptian, explains the Sun's Motion and Moon Phases.

The Sun is carried across the sky in a boat. At sunset it is swallowed by the Sky Goddess, and is reborn each morning. The Moon is attacked by a sow each month, and, after getting smaller and dimmer, it finally dies and then is reborn as a "new" Moon.

2. *The Traveling Sky Baskets* from the Apanyekra people of Brazil, explains how Sun and Moon came to the sky and how they avoid freezing or burning the earth.

Once Sun and Moon lived in a house on Earth among fields and trees. But they decided that the Earth was too crowded, so they each chose a path in the sky— Sun in day and Moon in night. But Sun burned the Earth the first day, and Moon froze it the first night. So, Sun and Moon decided to travel in baskets with lids. Sun didn't burn the Earth and Moon didn't freeze it. To this day, they still cross the sky in traveling baskets with lids.

3. *Anansi's Six Sons* West African and Haitian, explains how the Moon came to be in the sky.

Because Anansi's six skillful sons rescued him, he decided to reward them with a beautiful, bright light he had found in the forest. But the brothers argued and fought over the light. Nyame, the Sky God said, "Before the light came you lived peacefully together." He threw it high into the sky where the brothers could not reach it, and that was how the Moon came to be.

4. *The Truth About the Moon* African, explains the relative brightness and positions of the Sun and Moon.

At first, Mr. Sun and Mrs. Moon shone together all day. The people begged one of them to light up the night, so Mrs. Moon did. But she was just as bright and hot as Mr. Sun, so the Earth was too hot. Neither Mr. Sun nor Mrs. Moon were willing to dim their light. Then Mr. Sun tricked Mrs. Moon into falling in the river, which dimmed her light. She got so mad at him that she is forever chasing him across the sky.

5. *Maui Tames the Sun* Maori, explains why the Sun goes across the sky slowly.

Once the Sun always travelled across the sky very fast. The people didn't have enough hours of sunlight for all their duties. Maui went to the cave where the Sun comes out every morning. With the help of his brothers and others from the tribe, he caught the Sun in a net. Maui ran toward the Sun with his axe held high and told the Sun the people needed him to slow down. The Sun said he was so battered that he could only go slowly now anyway. Maui made him promise to do so, and then let him go.

The myths/stories above were adapted and summarized from the following resources: (1) *Ancient Cosmologies* by Carmen Blacker and Michael Loewe; (2) *Moon Was Tired of Walking on Air* by Natalia M. Belting; (3) *Legends of the Sun and Moon* by Eric and Tessa Hadley; (4) *The Truth About the Moon* by Clayton Bess; (5) *Land of the Long White Cloud* by Kiri Te Kanawa. See the Resources section for full reference listing.

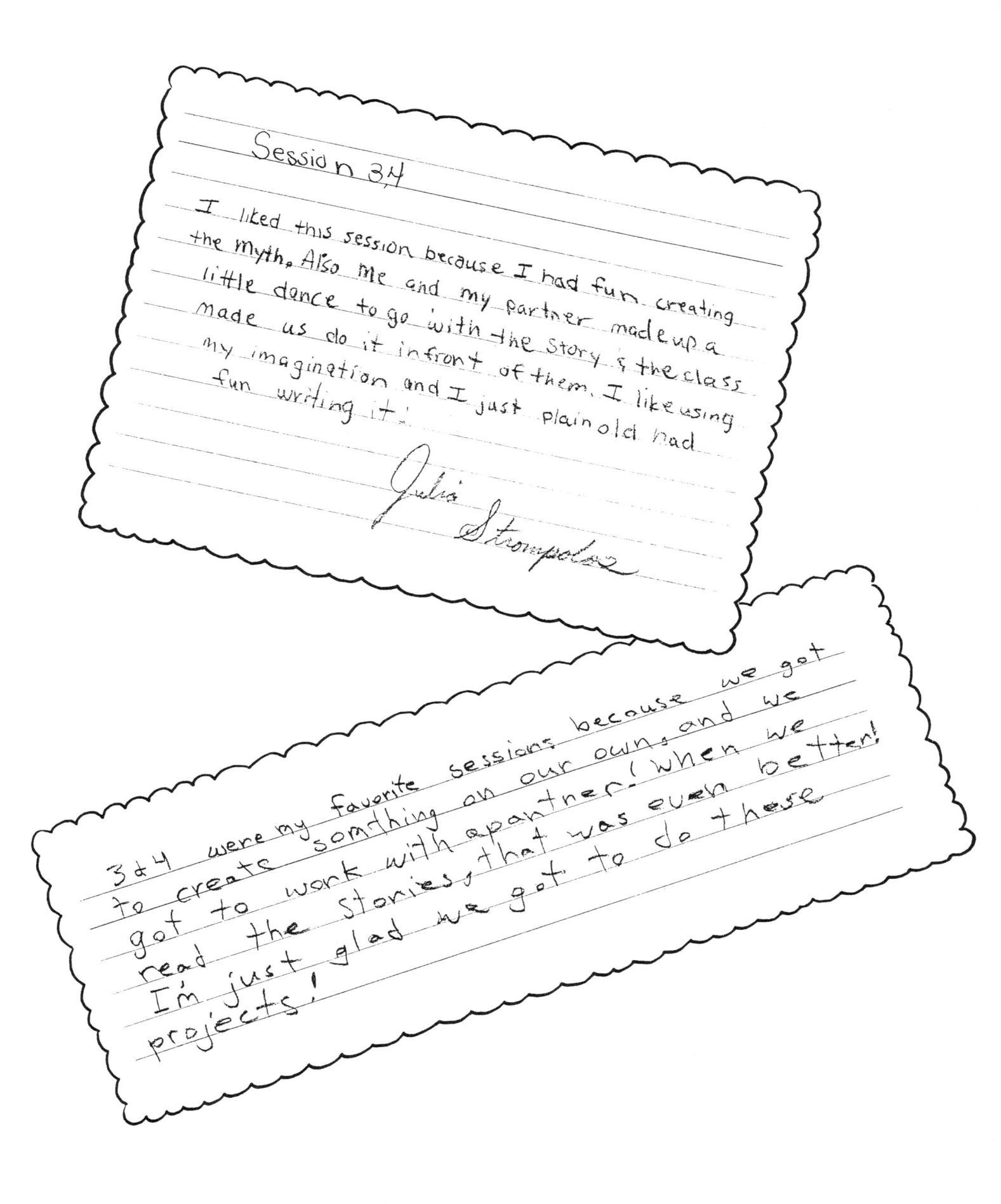

Session 3,4

I liked this session because I had fun creating the myth. Also me and my partner made up a little dance to go with the story & the class made us do it in front of them. I like using my imagination and I just plain old had fun writing it!

Julia Stroumpolos

3 & 4 were my favorite sessions because we got to create somthing on our own, and we got to work with a partner! When we read the stories, that was even better! I'm just glad we got to do these projects!

Session 5: Uncovering the Past or What's Hidden in the Midden?

Overview

Much of our knowledge about early human cultures comes from studying the objects they left behind. The science of archaeology often focuses on old village sites known as middens. Middens are deposits that people have left behind, the remains of settlements, the "garbage dumps" of long lost communities. We can infer many things about what people valued and the materials they used in daily life by studying objects such as bones, wood, and shells that have been preserved in middens.

In this session, students re-enact how human artifacts are deposited over time, by taking part in a role-play in which people from the past drop objects near a stream. Natural events are simulated, such as the accumulation of soil and autumn leaves falling over the objects. After a demonstration of the procedures that will be used to excavate the site, teams of students work together to excavate objects from layers of soil in shoe box "middens." As the Excavator carefully removes the objects from the leaves and soil, the Map Maker draws symbols representing the objects on a map. The Curator then makes a key to the objects on the map and categorizes the objects in a museum made from an egg carton.

Students learn that materials discarded or lost by people long ago can provide valuable clues for reconstructing a picture of an earlier culture. In a way, these materials, and what we can infer from them, are like puzzle pieces in an emerging image of a people's way of life. While practicing the methods of archaeologists, students infer information from objects, group the objects, and share drawings and explanations of clues from the past.

Native Culture, Archaeology & City Planning

In conjuction with the midden activities consider presenting a modern day city planning problem that could happen in your community: A large development company wants to build a shopping mall and has applied for a permit from the City Planning Commission. Many people in the community want this mall to be built; it will have all kinds of stores and offices and aid the local economy. But other members of the community oppose building the mall at that location because it is thought that the site was once a Native American village and may contain important information about that culture. Descendants of the local Indigenous people are demanding "repatriation" and the return of any remains or artifacts to the tribe. The City Planning Commission requests the help of a team of archaeologists from a nearby university to determine if Native Americans once lived at the site.

One fourth grade teacher used the middens activity in connection with a larger unit she regularly presents to several classes on "Indian Uses of the Earth." She had her students, working in groups, make three-layer middens themselves, discussing the possible uses of each item prior to burying it. After all middens were made, they were anonymously exchanged among the groups. Maps with grids were made for each layer. Items were collected in egg cartons and discussed. The students then did a creative writing activity, writing stories based on their findings and inferences. The teacher found that student experience making and analyzing the middens greatly aided their creative writing.

What You Need

For the Teacher/Class Demonstration (Stepping Back in Time)

Making the Middens

Stackable plastic shoe boxes are one excellent alternative to cardboard shoeboxes. While misting the cardboard boxes can weaken the sides of the shoeboxes, it's no problem with the plastic containers. Misting can be important to keep the layers from mixing, and also to reduce dust and thus minimize allergies.

It's worth emphasizing that while multiple layers are ideal, they are not absolutely necessary for the essence of the activity to get across For those who are doing the middens quickly, for teachers in teacher's workshops for example, using only soil may be more convenient, or one layer of soil, with leaves on top for a sense of layering. Those who want to re-use the same middens in different workshops or for other classes should of course be aware that once the layers become mixed, they cannot be easily unmixed. A final quick preparation tip in the case of middens with only one layer: it is possible to push artifacts down to varying depths into an already full box of topsoil when pressed for time, rather than placing them in during an assembly line process as generally recommended.

For younger students, you may choose to omit the sand layer.

After the activity, your students can use the excavated mixture of soil, sand and leaves to enrich a garden or to use in planters or terrariums.

For each group of 3 students:

❏ 1 shoe box midden (see "Making the Middens", and "Getting Ready," page 50.)
❏ tray or box for sifting or spooning soil into
❏ 1 stiff-bristle inexpensive paint brush or toothbrush (to remove soil above an artifact and to clean artifacts)
❏ 3 plastic spoons
❏ 1–2 plastic strawberry baskets to use as sifters
❏ 1 egg carton with the lid removed
❏ 1 ruler (optional)*
❏ 1 student sheet: "Archaeologist Checklist Task Cards" (master included, page 110)
❏ 3 pieces of 8-1/2 " x 14" white paper for mapping midden
❏ 1 piece of lined paper for making a key
❏ 3 pencils
❏ newspapers to cover table
❏ string about 18" long for making a grid (optional)*
❏ scissors to cut the string (optional)*
❏ tape to attach the string grids to the shoeboxes (optional)*

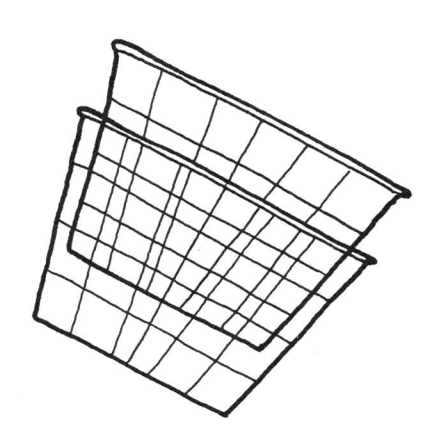

Putting two strawberry baskets together, one inside the other, will decrease the size of the holes and enable smaller objects to be sifted.

* Related to options described in the "Preparation" and "Selecting a Midden for Your Class" sections on the next three pages.

An Important Note about Preparation

The amount of time required to collect the materials and assemble the middens is considerable, especially the first time you teach it. Consider one or more of the following time savers:

•Use the sample letter to parents asking for materials (page 67).

•If you can, get help in assembling the middens. If you set up the shoe boxes and artifacts in an "assembly line," your midden building will go much more quickly. (See page 43.)

•Use the simulated artifacts again in future sessions.

•Have the "dig" activity outside, to minimize clean-up.

As mentioned earlier, this is a rewarding educational activity that engenders great student enthusiasm, prompting many teachers to say that, despite the preparation time and the mess, it is well worth it!

Selecting a Midden for Your Class

Please see the midden variations, drawings and boxed text on the next three pages for a description of various options. Remember, even the simplest of middens provides a great learning opportunity for your class!

It is important to read through Sessions 5 and 6 and the "Going Furthers" on page 63. Pay special attention to materials and preparation, in order to decide on the approaches you think most appropriate for your class. Options and alternatives regarding age range and complexity are also offered within the text.

Simplified Midden

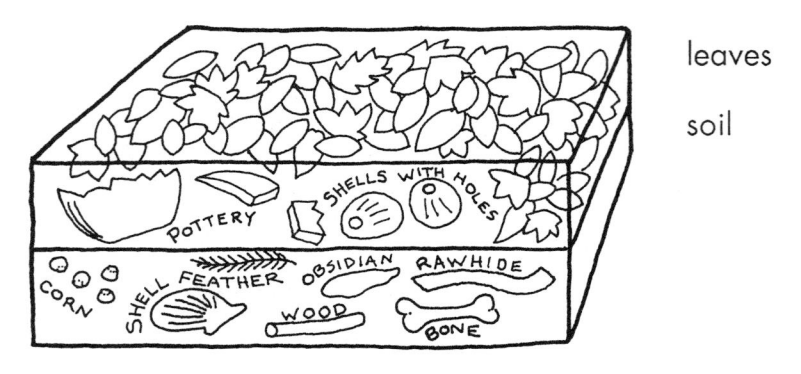

leaves

soil

Layer Cake Midden

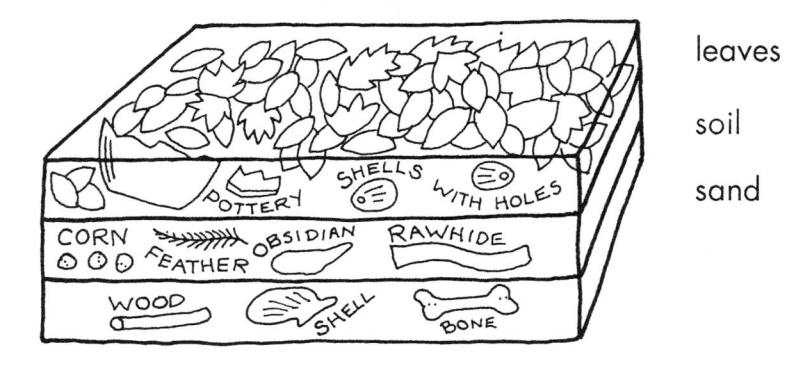

leaves

soil

sand

Items at the top show greater tool use and provide clues about more recent developments in technology. Items at the bottom are the least modified and are common to most ancient cultures.

Consider Extensions

Some teachers may want to extend the already rich midden activities in Sessions 5 and 6 even further. If you plan to add extensions, please read the "Going Further for Sessions 5 and 6" section on page 63, and adjust your preparation time accordingly. "Going Further" ideas include:

- **focusing on the societal and ethical aspects of plans to build a shopping mall on the site of an ancient Native American village or sacred burial site. What if the middens the class is excavating were found at such a site?**

- **an outdoor sandbox midden**

- **a play or other dramatic presentation**

- **a timeline**

ARRANGING THE MIDDENS

Some teachers have begun by arranging all the shoe box middens together in a rectangular or other shape, and numbering them, so the students can see where their portion fits into the larger "find." This has some nice advantages; even when a string grid is not used, it can give younger students a basic sense of a grid approach to mapping an area, thus conveying the archaeological need to keep careful track of the locations where objects are found. If you plan to group middens this way, it is desirable to use shoeboxes that are all the same size.

The making of a single large group map, in which students record objects found in their areas, is also an option in this case. Use a large sheet of butcher paper and trace the outline of each midden within it. Students can either draw directly on the group map, or tape their maps made at the table onto the appropriately numbered area on the group map.

Later, when students are discussing how what they found may have gotten there or what it may have been used for, they may also want to consider where within the larger "find" the objects were unearthed and how that might or might not relate to other objects found nearby. If a group map is used with older students who are mapping separate layers, they will need to make a map for each layer.

Middens: Some Variations...

The following midden options are offered to demonstrate how flexible the activity can be. Please feel free to mix and match the options as suits your time limitations, curricular needs, and grade level, and come up with adaptations of your own!

Number of Layers

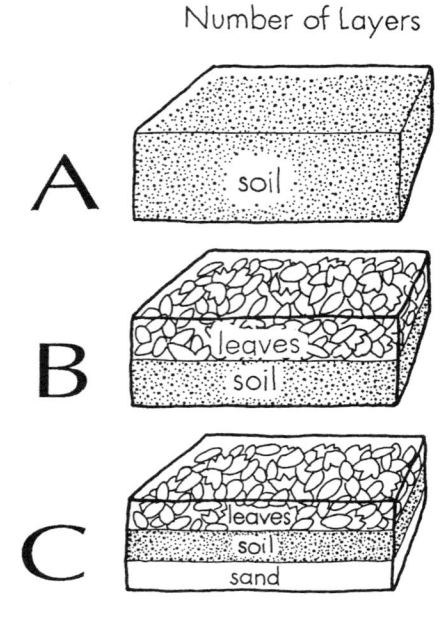

● **Number of Layers**

Within your shoebox middens, you can have one, two or three layers, depending on the age and abilities of your students. However many layers you choose to have, make each layer as thick as possible.

A. The Most Basic Midden • Only one layer, soil

B. The Medium Midden • Two layers, leaves and soil.

C. The Maximum Midden • Three layers: leaves, soil, and sand.

Grid Systems

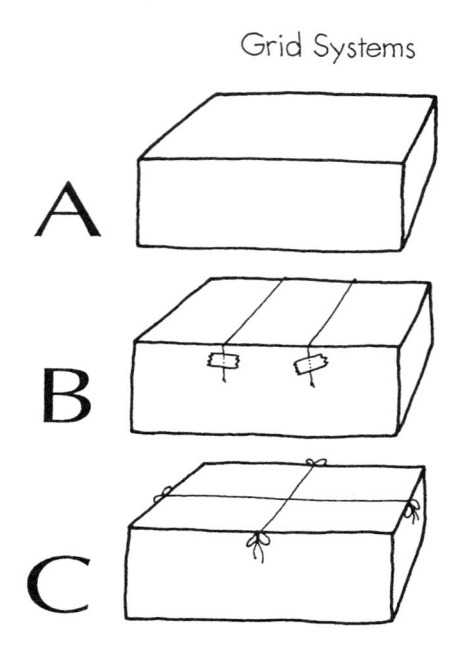

● **Use of String Grid System**

A. No grids.

B. Grids divide the midden into the areas where each student will dig.

C. A grid mapping system divides the midden into smaller areas for precision in recording where artifacts were found. Grid areas can be recorded and numbered on the map. Older students can put on grids themselves, using a ruler, tape and string.

.....for Your Consideration

● **MAPMAKING PROCEDURES**

A. One map for the whole midden. The Mapmaker uses one sheet of paper to draw or trace all of the artifacts found by the group in the appropriate locations.

B. A map for each layer of the midden. The Mapmaker uses a separate sheet of paper to map the artifacts in each layer of the midden.

C. One large class map. This could be a piece of butcher paper cut large enough to fit over all the middens placed together, with the separate middens outlined and numbered. See "Arranging the Middens," on page 47.

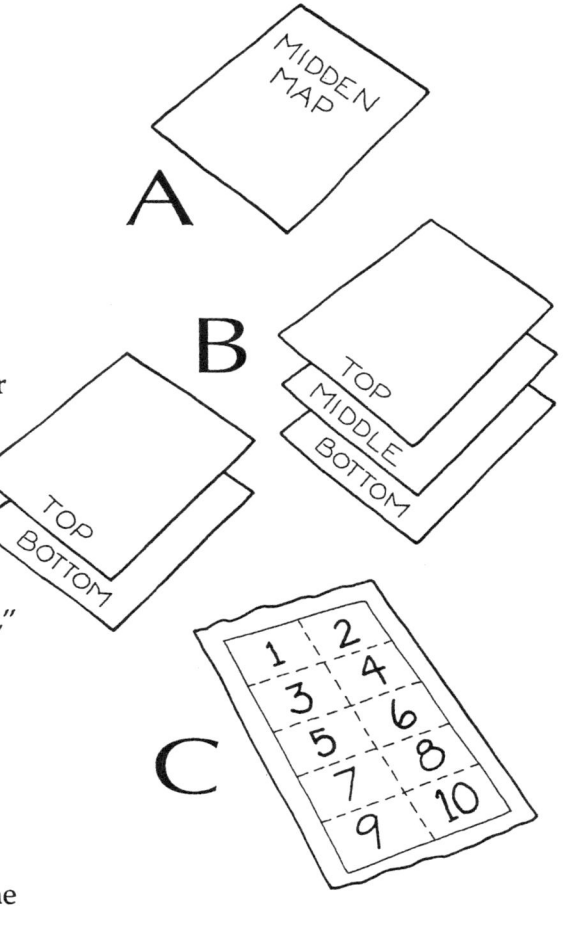

● **SANDBOX MIDDEN OPTION**

1. This option involves the use of a large raised sandbox or gardening box, or a small child's plastic swimming pool filled with sand/soil, as a class midden. The sand/soil must be clean. (If outside be sure there is a lid firmly covering it to prevent others from disturbing it or animals from soiling it.)

2. One sheet of butcher paper the size of the entire midden can be used as a "life-size" map for the entire class. A string grid system may be used to select areas of excavation for certain groups of students and/or as a mapping aid. Some teachers have done this with half the class at a time. The teacher defines the procedures for students to excavate and record.

3. With this option, layering would probably be restricted to one layer, either sand or soil, with an added surface layer of scattered leaves.

SWIMMING POOL as MIDDEN OPTION

Getting Ready Before the Day of the Activity

Planning the Middens

1. In the weeks before the activity, begin collecting materials for the middens. To enlist parent help, adapt the "Letter to Parents" on page 67. If possible, arrange to have some assistant(s) available to help you on the day you build your middens.

2. When you have collected the simulated artifacts, make a plan for where the objects will be placed in the shoe box middens. With a plan and an assembly line strategy, it will take one to two hours to make 10 middens. (The more help you have, the more quickly it will go!)

3. If you don't have ten of each artifact, you might plan to vary the middens. You might decide, for example, that some of the shoebox middens come from a certain area of the dig site. If only those middens have bones and burnt wood in the bottom layer, the students who excavate them may infer that their area of the ancient village site was used for cooking long ago.

4. You may plan to use the suggested layering below, or invent your own. There is no one right way to layer your middens.

One Plan for Layering Middens

Top layer (under leaves)	shells with holes suede or rawhide
Middle layer (soil)	pottery corn barley mat or string wood feathers obsidian
Bottom layer (sand)	burned wood clam shells chicken bones

5. For younger students, decide on ways to simplify the procedures. You might decide to have only one layer, using only potting soil. You may want to divide the midden box with string, and let each student have a section to excavate.

6. For older students, duplicate the Archaeologist Checklist Task Cards (page 57 or 110), and cut them into three task cards for each team.

Making the Middens

1. Set out the empty shoeboxes in a row. Put the shoe box bottoms into their lids to give the boxes added strength.

2. Count and sort the objects you have collected to be "artifacts." On the bottom of each midden, place the ones you have chosen to be buried deepest, then cover them with sand. You may then want to add another kind of object and cover with more sand. Lightly mist the top of the sand layer with water from a spray bottle and tamp down the sand. This slight amount of moisture will help keep the sand from shifting as you transport the boxes.

2. Place a different variety of objects in the middle layer of potting soil, sprinkle with water and tamp down the soil.

3. To stimulate student interest, arrange some especially interesting objects on the surface, and cover these with a layer of leaves.

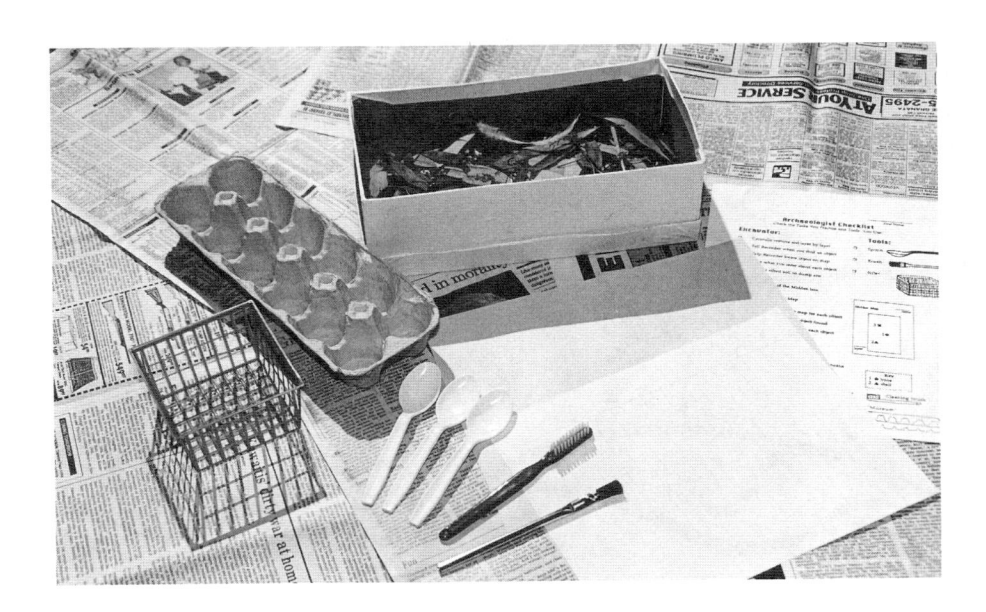

Getting Ready On the Day of the Activity:

1. Arrange the middens and materials in an area of the room where students can get them when you have finished the introductory demonstrations.

2. In the area where you plan to introduce the activity to the class, have your demonstration materials (a shoebox lid for a tray, soil, and leaves, and the three simulated artifacts) handy for the student role play, "Stepping Back in Time." Also have on hand a set of the tools to be used in the midden activity, the Archaeological Checklist task cards, and one midden to use as an example. Have the Midden Site Map ready to post after the role-play.

3. Decide how you want to form teams of students. One goal of the activity is to give students experience collaborating as a team of archaeologists. Group students who will work well together.

4. If students will be switching roles, you may want to identify the more patient students to start out as the Excavators. If you don't think groups can take turns agreeably, plan a system for switching roles. You might suggest, for instance, that they switch roles after each layer, or after the team has found a certain number of artifacts.

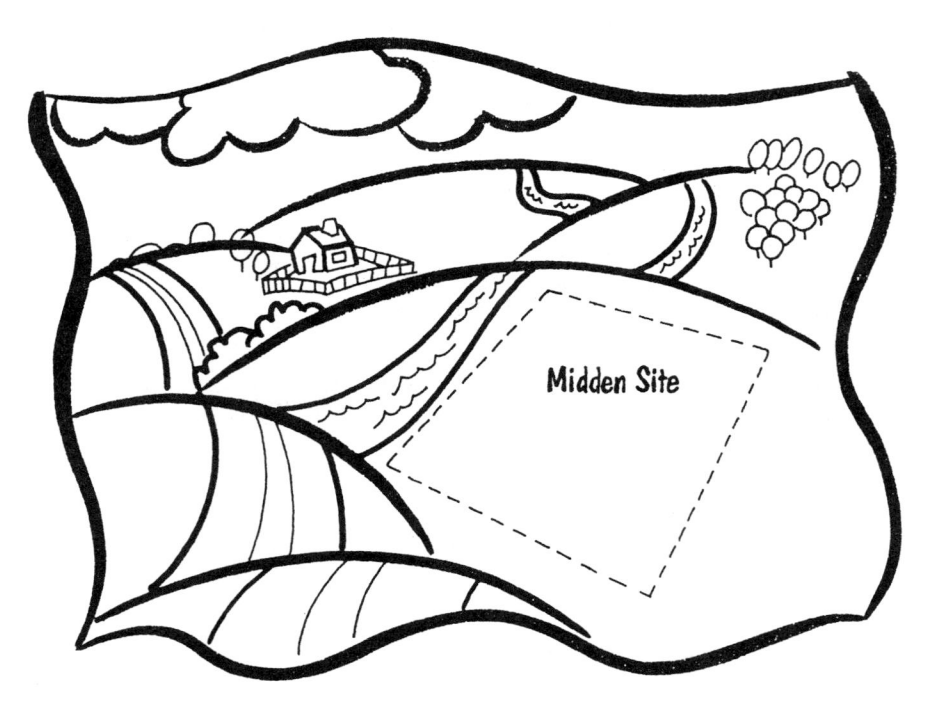

M I D D E N   S I T E

Stepping Back in Time: An Introductory Role-Play

1. Provide a link to the previous sessions by asking the class to describe some of the ways that scientists and other scholars learn about earlier human cultures. (In addition to describing the study of masks and myths, students may mention finding skeletons, tools, arrowheads, and houses.)

2. Invite three volunteers to come up to help dramatize the ways that objects from the past might have become buried.

Some teachers prefer to skip this dramatization of artifacts dropping over time. You know what is best for your class. Certainly when presenting this activity to other teachers, the dramatization is unnecessary and may seem overly contrived.

3. Ask the class to imagine that it's 2000 years ago. Say that the first volunteer is someone living in those long ago days who might have dropped something. Put the tray (shoe box lid) on a table where all can see, and sprinkle some soil in the tray to represent an area near a stream.

4. Give the first volunteer an object representing an old artifact, such as a simulated arrowhead or burnt piece of wood. Ask the volunteer to walk past the tray and leave the object somewhere on the soil. (As volunteers finish their roles, thank them and have them return to their seats.)

5. Ask the class to describe some natural ways that this object could become covered. [A volcano erupting, a landslide, the stream overflowing, etc.] Pour some soil over the object.

6. Ask the class to imagine that many years have passed. Identify a second volunteer as a person who visited the site about 50 years ago (perhaps the grandparent of a student). Give the volunteer an old penny or horseshoe to leave on the surface of the soil. Then simulate leaves falling over the years to cover the object.

7. Again ask the class to imagine that years have passed. Have the third volunteer represent someone from only last week who dropped a bottle cap on the surface of the leaves.

8. Ask, "If we were to dig here, where we might expect to find the oldest objects?" [In the deepest layers]

A midden map made by a first grader.

The key to the midden map above.

Introducing the Activity: Jobs of the Archaeologists

1. Ask students to imagine that the earth on the tray is located on a hillside that was once the site of a Native American village. Put up the picture of the Midden Site, and define a *midden* as a place in an ancient village site where objects have been left and become buried over time.

2. Explain that *archaeologists* are scientists who study the objects left behind by people in the past. This work often involves digging down through layers of earth in middens to find and study objects or *artifacts* from ancient human civilizations.

3. Say that archaeologists are respectful of past civilizations and want to learn as much as possible about them, so they work carefully together at three main tasks. Write the three tasks on the board: **Excavators** dig very carefully, **Map Makers** make maps and record where objects are found, and **Curators** label and preserve objects.

4. Tell the students that they are going to be archaeologists as they dig carefully into their middens. Like the story about the turtle and the hare, the lesson of "slow and steady wins the race" will greatly help their work. Careful and patient work has led to some great scientific discoveries. Explain that, before they start, they need to listen very closely to some very important tips for success.

5. Explain that students will be working in teams of three on each midden. Explain that they will share the three tasks either by agreeing to take turns or by following whatever system you have decided upon. Use the materials to demonstrate briefly the tools and techniques the students will use:

> •The **Map Maker** first makes a map of the "dig site" by tracing the shape of the midden on the paper. Mention that the Map Maker won't need to draw exact pictures of the objects the team finds. A circle can represent a coin, for example. If they find another coin, they can use the same symbol again. Younger students may prefer to trace some of the objects. Older students can make a separate map for each layer of the midden.

> •The **Excavator** carefully works on one layer of the midden with the spoon, brush and sifter (rather than

digging a hole to the bottom), until an object is uncovered. Before the Excavator takes the object out of the midden, she alerts the team so the Map Maker can determine where it should be drawn on the map. You will probably also want to stress that while they will dig downward slowly, they also need to carefully examine all across each layer.

The strawberry baskets may be used as sifters to remove small objects. Excavators can get teammates' help sifting and removing soil into the trays and sliding the soil off these trays into a large bucket (or trash bag) as the soil accumulates. (Put one basket inside another so smaller artifacts can be found.)

• The **Curator** cleans the objects with a brush, numbers and groups them with other similar objects in the "egg carton museum." The Curator also makes a key that tells what each of the Map Maker's symbols means.

6. Have students form teams of three, and ask the teams to cover their tables with newspaper.

7. For older students, hand out the Archaeologist Checklist Task Cards. Be sure each group knows how they will share the tasks before allowing them to get their midden. Ask teams to send a Curator to pick up the middens and equipment when they are ready to begin.

The Activity: Digging into the Past

1. Circulate among teams, assisting with questions and encouraging collaboration and sharing of tasks. Bring the dump buckets or bags with you to each table to remove the excavated soil.

2. Encourage Excavators to be careful and go slowly, so as not to miss an artifact or mix layers.

3. With older students, remind Map Makers to make a new map when their team comes to a new layer of artifacts. (The leaves on top count as the top layer.) Ask questions like, "Which objects do you think are from longer ago? How do you know?"

With all students, it is important to stress lateral exploration as well as downward excavation. One complete (horizontal) layer should be removed at a time, taking care not to disturb the layer underneath. Rushed vertical digging could move or damage artifacts in lower layers.

4. Some students, especially the younger ones, may finish their excavations in five to ten minutes. Older students have sometimes taken 20 or 30 minutes. Encourage students who finish early to compare and describe or sketch the simulated artifacts. If two teams finish early, have them compare their findings.

5. Once the teams have completed their excavations and cleaned up the excess soil, explain that in the next session, the class will discuss what has been found at the dig site.

6. Have each group make sure their names are on their maps and egg cartons, and then put them in a central storage area.

ARCHAEOLOGIST CHECKLIST TASK CARDS
Check the Tasks and Tools

Check the Tasks You Do and Tools You Use   _____ (name)

Excavator:

☐   Carefully remove soil layer by layer

☐   Tell Map Maker when you find an object

☐   Remove sifted soil to dump bag

Tools:

☐   Spoon

☐   Brush

☐   Sifter

Check the Tasks You Do and Make a Map   _____ (name)

Map Maker:

☐   Make a map of the Midden box

☐   Draw or trace each object on the map

☐   Write the name of the object

Midden Map

Shell

Bone

Wood

Check the Tasks You Do and Tools You Use   _____ (name)

Museum Curator:

☐   Help the Map Maker decide where to draw an object

☐   Clean off each object found

☐   Group similar objects in the egg carton

Tools:

☐   Cleaning Brush

☐   "Museum"

Session 6: Putting Together Clues from the Past

Overview

n this session, students list and describe the different kinds of objects uncovered in each midden. Once all of the objects have been listed on the chalkboard, students are asked to brainstorm ways the objects may have been used by the people who lived at the site hundreds or thousands of years ago.

During the discussion, students are encouraged to compare their findings and share their further inferences with other teams. Students then return to their teams and each person selects one object from the team "museum" to study further. Students sketch their objects, list possible uses and other inferences and draw a picture of how the object might have been used by the past culture. Depending on the time available, these individual reports may be shared orally or displayed in writing as part of the "artifact museum."

One 5th grade teacher said that after the middens activity, "50% of my class now want to be archaeologists—if I weren't a teacher, I'd be out on a dig."

What You Need

For the class:
- ❏ large map of the midden site showing hill, stream, trees (optional)
- ❏ chalkboard or large paper for recording ideas
- ❏ marker to write names of artifacts on the cards
- ❏ pocket chart for organizing the objects into categories (optional)
- ❏ about 30 blank cards that fit into the pocket chart (optional)
- ❏ masking tape (optional)

Use of a "pocket chart" is optional. Some teachers have found it a handy organizational tool for this activity. Others prefer to write on the board, especially when many different ideas are being suggested in rapid fashion. If you do use a pocket chart, make sure it has plenty of pockets!

For each group of 3 students:
- ❏ maps of midden artifacts made in Session 5
- ❏ 1 egg carton containing the team's artifacts
- ❏ 3 pieces of 8 1/2" x 11" paper for describing an artifact
- ❏ 3 pencils
- ❏ 1 ruler

Getting Ready

1. Make sure the students have the maps and egg carton museums ready for the discussion.

2. Read through the session and determine the most stimulating way for your class to sum up and analyze their "findings." Sometimes the class has become so involved in the middens activity that anything afterward seems anti-climactic. Other classes thrive on both the sorting and classification discussion and the controversy about the possible uses of artifacts, and the teacher's task then becomes keeping the comments relatively brief and the entire class involved in wide-ranging discussion.

3. You know the interests and dynamics of your class best. With younger students, for example, you may want to consider picking only three or four artifacts for the class discussion. This discussion will then provide students with some examples of what they are asked to do when they focus on a single artifact. With older students, careful and complete classification of their findings and debate about the intricacies of evaluating inferences can greatly enliven the discussion.

4. Some teachers like using a pocket chart; others prefer the flexibility of the chalkboard. If you decide to use a pocket chart and artifact cards to record the possible categories of use for the artifacts, have the artifact cards ready as well. Decide in advance whether you will write the names of the artifacts on the cards or have students write (or draw) them during the discussion.

Discussing What Was Hidden in the Middens

1. Have students gather in their midden groups and pass out their egg carton museums and maps. Let them have a few minutes to re-examine and discuss their finds.

2. Gather the attention of the whole class. Begin with a very open discussion, encouraging students to talk about any surprises, controversies and ideas. After their initial comments and reactions, guide the discussion toward the subject of teamwork and how it felt to be archaeologists collaborating on a project.

Especially with older students, you may want to discuss the very important fact that our inferences about other cultures are limited, not only by partial evidence, but also by the assumptions and values of our own cultures. Our own ingrained patterns and ways of looking at things may often prevent us from understanding assumptions and practices of others that may be quite different from our own, even sometimes leading to completely unwarranted or distorted conclusions.

For younger students, keep the categories simple, and the discussions brief. You may want to focus directly on the properties of some of given objects, rather than what scientists might further infer from them.

You may also want to write the numbers of the middens in which the artifacts appeared. This will encourage teams to compare their findings. It also could tie in with the Mall construction scenario, if you are including that as part of this activity.

3. Focus the group on the nature of the objects collected by asking students to help you list on the chalkboard (or on the pocket chart) all of the different kinds of artifacts uncovered. Tell students to refer to their museums for input to the class list. For review, ask which objects are from longer ago—those in the top or the bottom layer?

4. Ask if there were differences between beads or bones or feathers that might be important. For example, some students may have found shells with holes in them, while other shells lacked holes. What could have caused these holes? [Some holes are made by the natural predators of mollusks, but some holes, especially irregular ones, can indicate that people drilled the shells to make jewelry.]

Artifact and Inference

1. Once you have the artifacts listed down one side of the chalkboard (or on the pocket chart cards), ask students to suggest some possible uses for the objects and/or add some of your own suggestions as need be. Write these as headings across the top of the chalkboard, such as Food, Cookware, Clothing, Jewelry, Housing, Weapons, etc.

2. Invite students to infer what uses the various artifacts may have had and list the artifact (or put a check) in the appropriate column or columns. Some artifacts may be placed in more than one category. For example, a piece of rawhide could be used for both clothing and jewelry. Encourage creative discussion of possible uses. (If using a pocket chart, invite students to come up and place an "artifact card" in the appropriate column or columns on the pocket chart. Artifacts with multiple uses will require multiple cards.)

3. Ask, "If we pretend that the middens were real, what could we guess about the lives, customs, eating habits and environment of the people who left these items behind?" Encourage students to support or dispute their inferences. You may want to remind students to listen to each other carefully, because the ideas of everyone are needed to come up with all the possibilities and refine conclusions.

4. Explain that archaeologists often disagree, since they can't be sure of what it was like long ago. Encourage students to discuss whether a particular inference is farfetched or supported by observable evidence. You may want to give a few

If you are including the context of the Mall, allow time to address the dilemma faced by the City Council. Is there sufficient evidence of a past human culture at the site to delay building? Who should decide what to do about the midden? How much does the company's ownership of the land affect the decision? Are there any compromises that can be reached? Should the land and/or the artifacts be returned to Tribal descendants? Why or why not? (One group of students suggested that the company pay for the archaeological investigation, then create a museum within the Mall for the community.)

examples of your own, including one or more obvious fabrications or unsupported assumptions, and ask for their comments.

5. Point out that what we know about modern people can sometimes help us make inferences about the past. For example, since people today still use shells in jewelry, mask-making, and weaving, maybe some of the shells in the middens were used that way. The evidence we muster in support of an inference can include findings from the past and knowledge from our own time, but there are many things about the past that we cannot know for certain.

Focusing on a Single Artifact

1. Ask students to select one artifact from their team's museum to sketch and write about. Tell them to list some of the inferences they can make about the object, then draw a picture of how people may have used the object in the past.

2. After students have had 15–20 minutes to work on their artifact reports, convene the class to share reports, or display the reports on the wall or as part of a book, where all can see and enjoy them.

Josh

6/6/91

Arrowhead

The arrowhead was found in Berkeley where a mall was going to be built.

This is how the arrowhead could have been used.

Going Further (for Sessions 5 and 6)

1. Enrich the skit "Stepping Back in Time" by having students spend some time preparing a play, with props and outfits appropriate to the time periods. There could be a time chart that shows events such as the year of birth of students, the founding of your school's town, invention of the automobile, and early history of the state. If students have pursued a study of local Native American cultures, invite them to enrich the drama with their findings.

2. For older students in particular, introduce important issues of social relevance, cultural clash, and controversy by supposing that the midden site has been unearthed during construction of a planned shopping mall. Assign or have students choose to represent different characters, each concerned with the fate of the midden/mall. Some of the characters may include: archaeologists, Native American representatives from the region, small business leaders (who are planning shops within the Mall), the Vice President of the corporation who owns the land, the Mayor, and so on. After allowing for research and preparation time, the class could conduct a town meeting, with a moderator (who may be the teacher).

3. Have students make shoe box middens for other classes and/or challenge classmates to excavate and interpret the new middens.

4. Bring in "mystery objects" from the past, such as a quill pen or a slide rule. Would your students know what they were if they uncovered these items at a dig? What inferences do they inspire?

5. Add a discussion or written assignment: What might people of the future guess about our culture if they uncovered a midden and found the contents of a box of toys? A video arcade? A refrigerator? A clothes closet? A trash bag? What does our garbage tell us about our culture?

Some North American Archæological Sites & Excavations

Center for American Archaeology is a research and teaching facility at a 12,000 year old site in the lower Illinois River Valley. You need to make an appointment to visit or become a volunteer there. Contact: Kampsville Archaeological Center, PO Box 365, Kampsville, Illinois 62053. (618) 653-4395.

Chippewa National Forest sites in Minnesota and Wisconsin date from 10,000 years ago through the late 17th century. Visitors do not need appointments but should contact this address for directions: Archaeological Outreach Program, University of Minnesota, 10 University Drive, Duluth, Minnesota 55812. (218) 726-7154.

Crow Canyon Center for Southwestern Archaeology is at an Anasazi pueblo site in southwestern Colorado. It is a research and teaching facility. Visitors are welcome, and volunteers may work there by arrangement. Contact: 23390 Country Road K, Cortez, Colorado 81321. (303) 565-8975 . Ute Mountain Tribal Park and the Mesa Verde National Monument are in the same general region.

Dogan Point Shell Midden is on the Hudson River just north of New York City, and is the oldest Atlantic coast mound north of Panama. Visitors are welcome. Appointments are required for guided tours. Volunteers are accepted for work on the excavation. The address: Department of Anthropology, Appalachian State University, Boone, North Carolina 28608.

Elden Pueblo is a pueblo site that is being stabilized and re-excavated in a participatory program involving 4th–9th grade students and family groups.Visitors are welcome. The address is: c/o Coconino National Forest, 2323 East Greenlaw Lane, Flagstaff, Arizona 86004. (602) 527-7410.

Mitchell Prehistoric Indian Village is a national archeological landmark. It is a fortified Plains Indian village dating from the 11th century with a museum, walk-through re-created lodge, and visitor's center. No appointment is necessary and volunteers are accepted. The address is P.O. Box 621, Indian Village Road, Mitchell, South Dakota, 57301. (605) 996-5473.

The Jones Site in Canada is an undisturbed and unplowed Huron village. Write for an appointment to visit the site with a guide. Some volunteers occasionally accepted. Address: Huronia Museum, Little Lake Park, P.O. Box 638, Midland, Ontario L4R 4P4 Canada.

There are numerous other sites throughout the United States and Canada. Many museums also offer archaeological programs. The *Archaeology Handbook* by Bill McMillon includes the above and many more, lists books on key topics in archaeology, and provided much of the information on these two resource pages. See the Resources section under "Archaeology" for a full listing for this book.

A Few World Archaeological Sites & Milestones

Dundee Bay Site is a Lucayan village (the Lucayos, Tainos, and Carib peoples were the first Indigenous peoples encountered by Columbus in the Caribbean) on the South Coast of Grand Bahama island. It is one of the largest open-air sites in the Bahamas. Volunteers over 21 years old accepted. Contact: Julian Granberry, P.O. Box 398, Horseshoe Beach, Florida 32648.

The Monte Alban Project in Mexico is excavating portions of a city thought to be built by the Zapotec people 2500 years ago. Recent excavations have traced human habitation in the region back 11,000 years. Volunteers and students are accepted. Contact: Instituto Nacional de Anthropologia e Historia en Oaxaca, Pino Suarez 715, Centro, C.P., 6800 Oaxaca, Oaxaca, Mexico.

Gordion is a site in Turkey whose history spans from the early Bronze Age to Roman times, with excavations primarily in the time of King Midas. It is southwest of Ankara, between two villages, and no appointment is necessary to visit. Contact: Kenneth Sims, Department of Classics, 212 Murphey Hall, University of North Carolina, Chapel Hill, North Carolina 27599-3145.

Tombs of the Kings is in the town of Paphos on the southwest coast of Cyprus. It was inhabited as early as the Chalcolithic period and reached prominence in the Late Bronze Age. No appointment is necessary and volunteers are accepted. Contact: Cyprus Museum, Nicosia, Republic of Cyprus. Telephone: 02303185.

Kasfiki, Kokotos, and Palaiopolis are sites in Corfu, Greece near the harbor of ancient Corfu. No appointment is necessary to visit. Volunteers should be college age. Contact: c/o Martha Joukowsky, P.O. Box 1837, Brown University, Providence, Rhode Island 02912. (401) 863-3188.

Dysart is a site in County Kilkenny, Ireland, including ruins from the 13th, 15th, and 17th centuries. Visitors need an appointment and volunteers must share a portion of excavation costs. Contact: Department of Anthropology, Kroeber Hall, University of California, Berkeley, California 94720. (415) 642-3391.

There are many other sites and excavations throughout the world. The modern science of archaeology developed as "famous finds" were made, starting in the late 1700s. In 1870 Heinrich Schliemann, a German businessman, began excavations of the city of Troy in what is now Turkey; prehistoric cave paintings were found in Spain in 1879; the royal cemetery near Qus, Egypt was excavated in 1894; excavations of the Minoan civilization on Crete began in 1900; and the discovery of King Tut's tomb in Egypt in 1922 sparked worldwide interest in archaeology. Milestones since then have included: discovery of flint points in Folsom, New Mexico indicating human settlement in North America many thousands of years ago (more recent discoveries and linguistic evidence push this estimate back many more thousands); remains and implements of very early human beings in Africa and Asia, the Dead Sea Scrolls, excavations of an ancient community in Jericho, Jordan, led by Dame Kathleen Kenyon, a British archaeologist; the discovery of an ancient civilization in what is now Syria, and the opening of the Ming Tombs and other Imperial sites in China.

he book *Motel of the Mysteries* (see Resources Listing under "Archaeology" for a full reference) is an excellent literary and scientific accompaniment to this unit and any unit that focuses on the collection of clues and evidence from which to make inferences, draw conclusions, or solve mysteries. This brilliantly conceived and carefully designed book takes place in the future and begins with the proposition that late 20th century civilization has been buried under an avalanche of paper, mostly direct mail advertising fliers, and much about the life of this lost era is not known until 4022. Only scanty evidence has been pieced together, including some remnants of the "imposing Temples of Bigapple," until a previously obscure individual named Howard Carson accidentally stumbles upon the "Motel of the Mysteries," whose contents and interpretations of their roles in the culture are displayed in the book.

The incredibly and bizarrely archaeological twists put upon interpretations of common household items, including toilet seats and other bathroom accessories, are stated in an academic, logical tone, as if they make perfect sense as final conclusions, yet we know that they are wildly and sometimes hilariously off the mark. The toilet bowl becomes the "sacred urn" of the "inner chamber," thought to be "carved from a single piece of porcelain and then highly polished." The archaeologists of the future believe that "the Urn was the focal point of the burial ceremony. The ranking celebrant, kneeling before the Urn, would chant into it while water from the sacred spring flowed in to mix with sheets of Sacred Parchment." The toilet seat itself is believed to have been a "sacred collar" worn by the "ranking celebrant" and secured to the urn after the ceremony. As for the "Sacred Parchment..."

Your students will no doubt appreciate both the down-to-earth humor and linguistic sophistication of this book. You could consider having students list or make a chart showing a possible inference process that the scholars of the future could have used to come to their conclusions. Ask them to think of reasons why it was believed a "burial chamber" was discovered. What was the evidence? Are there other interpretations? How does this process compare to the one students used in the GEMS activities? Is it possible that their proposed inferences are just as far afield as the interpretations in *Motel of the Mysteries*?

You could also have your students do some research on a famous archaeological discovery, such as the ancient tombs of Egyptian pharoahs or Chinese emperors, or the numerous sites closer to home. Have any early assumptions or conclusions about these cultures been shown to be false? Are there differences in interpretation or controversies about the meaning of the findings?

For a creative finale to this investigation, why not have your students work in teams to write and illustrate their own versions of a book similar to *Motel of the Mysteries*, focusing perhaps on the future discovery of a school and a classroom a lot like your own! ●

Sample Letter for Midden Materials

Dear Parents,

As part of a unit called, "Investigating Artifacts," your child's class will soon model the work of archaeologists. In archaeology, a "midden" is defined as a place where people who lived before have left things behind. Instead of real middens, students will investigate simulated middens, made from shoe boxes.

Inside each midden, different layers of soil will represent different time periods and various "artifacts" will provide clues to the past. This activity can help students develop respect and appreciation for ancient peoples, while learning and practicing scientific processes.

There are many things that we need for this project, so we are asking for your help. Please see if you have any of the following items, or if you know others who do. It will be appreciated if your donations are clean. We will need to have these materials by_____.

(date)

- adult-sized shoeboxes (about 6" wide and 12" long) with lids
- potting soil (without styrofoam beads or vermiculite)
- clean sand
- shells
- unglazed clay pots
- chicken bones
- unpopped popping corn
- dried beans
- small pieces of obsidian rock (not sharp)
- small burned and unburned pieces of wood
- suede leather or rawhide (natural colors)
- small pieces of woven grass mat or string (natural colors)
- feathers (not artificially colored)
- an old coin, horseshoe or arrowhead
- an empty spray bottle
- small, stiff-bristle paint brushes
- plastic spoons
- plastic strawberry baskets
- egg cartons

Please let me know if you have time one afternoon to help assemble the shoebox middens. **Thank you very much!**

Going Further (for the entire unit)

1. Hold a "Storytelling Sharing" for other classes, at a parent's night, or other event, at which student stories from the unit are dramatized, and masks and midden artifacts displayed. Invite one or more Native-American and/or children's storytellers or folksingers. Branch out from the anthropological and archaeological emphases of the unit to explore the literary and social studies aspects of learning more about present-day Native American cultures, concerns, and aspirations.

2. Extend the "museum" concept to include the entire unit. Have students create one large museum that includes objects excavated from the middens as well as student drawings, myths and masks. Invite other classes for a "tour" and make it a prominent display for parent's night.

3. Have your students obtain oral histories from their parents, grandparents, neighbors or friends, comparing the present with the past. Provide students with research topics, such as Food, Clothing, or Shelter. Students can ask for permission to write down or record their interview questions and answers. This could fit into larger oral history projects in your school district or region and people who work on those projects could be invited to the classroom.

4. Ask students to imagine that a highly intelligent being from a planet in a distant solar system is suddenly transported to Earth, and lands right in the middle of our schoolyard during recess. The being is only able to stay until the bell rings, and then will be returned to the distant planet. Have students list 10 things the outer-space observer might see, feel, hear, touch, or taste, or intuit. When the being returns to the distant planet, others there ask what kind of culture exists on Earth. Write down five things the being might conclude about our culture and society (inferences that might be made). For extra credit, have students draw this being, either in the schoolyard, or back on the planet giving a report to other inhabitants, or both! This could be a whole class activity, done in teams, or used as part of an individual student assessment activity.

5. Celebrate your "Masks, Myths, and Middens" unit with a cake made up of different colored/flavored layers, filled with surprises between the layers, inserted after cooling (gummy bears, circus cookies, etc.).

Mystery Objects
Teachers can select **unfamiliar** *"mystery objects." These objects are often found in kitchens, garages or classroom closets, or at the local "goodwill" store. These objects should be sturdy and safe to handle. Ask students to closely examine the object and write individually about the following questions:*

1. Use words and pictures to describe your object in detail.

2. How could people have used this object in the past?

3. Why do you think people used the object that way?

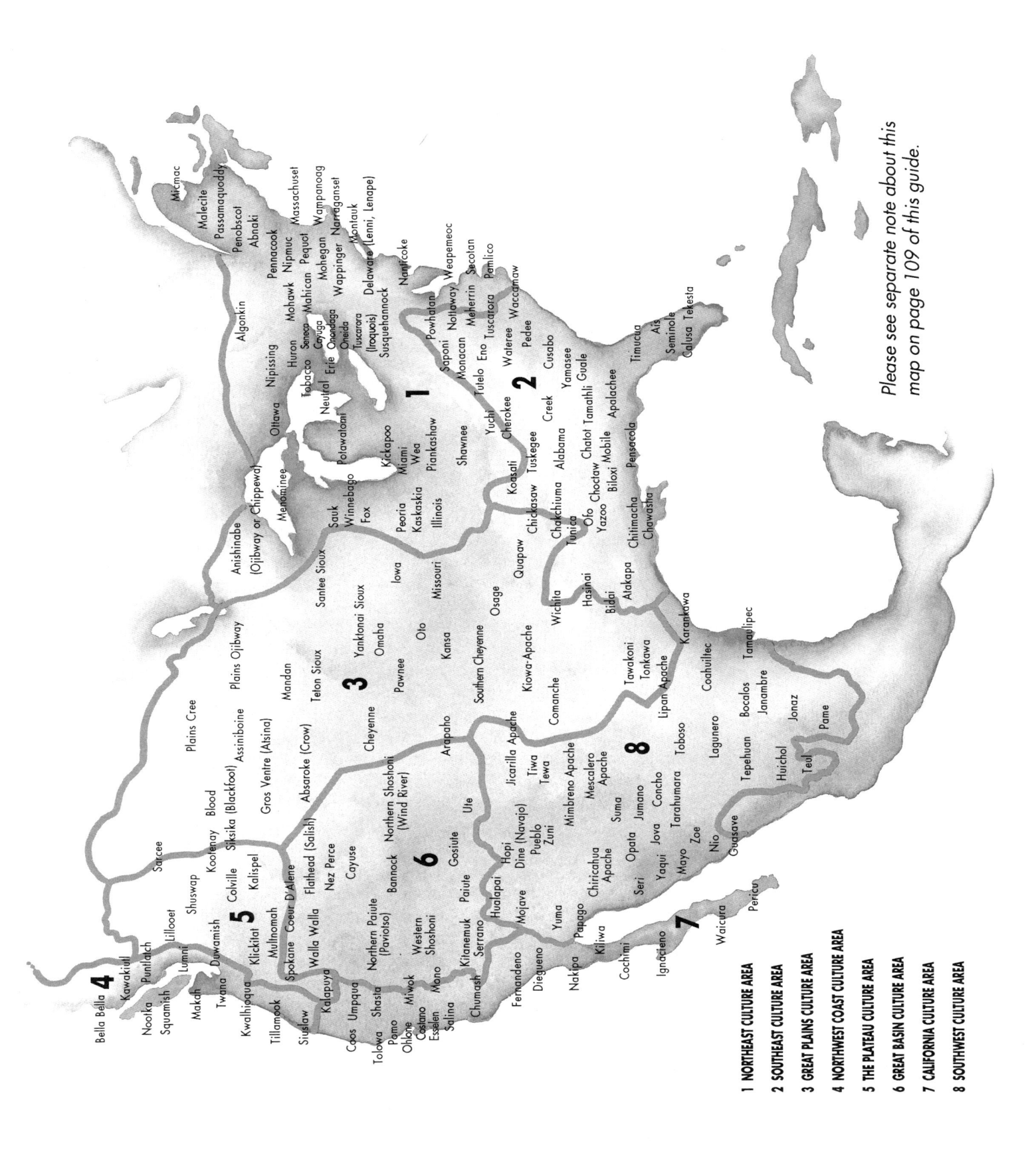

Please see separate note about this map on page 109 of this guide.

1 **NORTHEAST CULTURE AREA**

2 **SOUTHEAST CULTURE AREA**

3 **GREAT PLAINS CULTURE AREA**

4 **NORTHWEST COAST CULTURE AREA**

5 **THE PLATEAU CULTURE AREA**

6 **GREAT BASIN CULTURE AREA**

7 **CALIFORNIA CULTURE AREA**

8 **SOUTHWEST CULTURE AREA**

Background for Teachers

The study of Native American issues, past and present, can be of great importance to **all** students' understandings of their own cultures and of U.S. history in general, providing a basis for further learning about the original and living inhabitants of the lands we now all occupy. Many elementary school curricula now contain some focus on Native American cultures.

The social science issues raised by learning more about Native American cultures and histories can enrich many areas of the curriculum. Depending on grade level and your other curriculum priorities, you may choose to introduce the present-day efforts of Indian peoples to establish sovereignty and treaty rights, battle discrimination, improve living conditions, and pass on, protect, and celebrate their unique ways of life. These issues also relate to global environmental matters and our human responsibilities to live "in harmony with Mother Earth."

Societal concerns regarding preservation of historical sites as well as issues relating to Native American burial sites and the storage by museums of Indian remains and artifacts also arise. The powerful resurgence of Native American activism and cultural affirmation, new emphases on the role multi-national and multicultural education must play for our society to live in harmony, the growth of worldwide environmental movements, and the debates raised by the 500th anniversary of Columbus's landing—all provide many opportunities for learning. As Jack Weatherford, whose excellent book *Indian Givers* summarizes contributions of Native Americans to the world in many fields, expressed it, "Columbus arrived in the New World in 1492, but America has yet to be discovered."

In recent years, increasing cultural sensitivity, along with improved written resources, have begun to counter the unfortunately stereotypical, simplistic, and often insulting portrayals of Native Americans found in many books, films, and children's games. **One important tool against stereotyping is the recognition of the diversity among Native Americans, giving specific context and detail whenever possible.** Pointing out the particular nation, confederation, or tribe who originated a particular myth, rather than lumping all "Indians" together is one good way to do this. Reading out loud and recommending to others some of the wonderful books now available can greatly assist this important educational process. It's also true that there are aspects of ecological practice and spiritual wisdom that bridge across many different Native American peoples—in this sense you could explore the theme of diversity and unity.

For many important reasons, a deeper understanding of the histories, lives, and national rights of Native peoples is on numerous agendas. We hope this guide makes its small but positive contribution. In turn, such a study opens up new vistas for positive and respectful explorations by all students of the lives and cultures of the many diverse peoples, including their own, whose achievements and experiences have contributed to our multicultural present.

The Meanings of Myth

It's important to recognize from the start that the Native American myths we draw on in this unit, like the myths of many other peoples, derive from a history of many thousands of years. With students of a certain age, you may want to make this distinction directly, noting that while the students are asked to create their own "myths," in fact the real process is a collective one that extends over many years of experience and oral tradition.

Ancient peoples everywhere observed the wonders, mysteries, and dangers of the world around them, and speculated about the forces at work. Many gave further meaning to what they observed by attributing events to spiritual entities representing natural forces. In observing and being part of change, people also sought answers to their questions about the future in patterns of past events, or in the movements of the stars and planets, or in other natural signs or human visions and intuitions.

Scientists also make inferences to explain their observations of the world, and they refine their inferences through testing and further observations. Myths contain different, less testable ideas expressed in beautiful and elaborate images and metaphors. Myths provide a philosophical framework for bringing meaning to a vast and chaotic universe. They are ways of looking at the world. They contain possible explanations for the actions and reactions of natural phenomena.

Refined by generations of spiritual leaders and storytellers, myths also reflect a great richness of language and creative expression. They often include powerful images and compelling dramatic tension. They can provide symbolic representations of natural phenomena or dynamics in human relations. They are *memorable*; they have been remembered by storytellers and shamans, healers and teachers, priests and planters. They contain lessons for human behavior that are passed on as part of the culture and its traditions, from parent to child. Myths also possess generous shares of emotional connection and wisdom; they give profound insight into both the specific culture from which they derive and the human experience in general.

There is a more narrow usage and definition of the word "myth," meaning something that is not true. A science educator, for example, might talk about gearing a lesson on dinosaurs to breaking down certain "myths," such as the all-too-prevalent notion that prehistoric cave people and dinosaurs co-existed. While this more negative meaning of the word "myth" has its purposes, our emphasis in this guide is on the larger sense of the word, on the much more positive sense of myth as a story or legend that explains the relationship between a people and the natural world, and that passes on lessons, beliefs, and meaning to future generations. The study of myths is called *mythology*. You may want to discuss the positive meaning of "myth" with your students, or consider other words to communicate the main idea.

Native American Storytelling

Introducing the word "myth" also coincides with the more elevated, respectful status given the word in English usage, as when we speak of Greek or Roman "myths," the study of "mythology" by scholars like Joseph Campbell, and the use of myths as threads of meaning that connect world cultures, seen by many as deeply important in understanding the global human psyche. Native American oral (and increasingly written) and storytelling traditions are certainly worthy of comparable linguistic (and cultural) respect. As noted in the text, however, if you consider the term "myth" disrespectful, judgmental, problematic, or confusing, consider other language, for example, "oral narratives" or "stories."

In English, and in current usage, the simple word "story" can sometimes be taken in a superficial way. Yet these are definitely "stories," and stories have great power in all cultures. **"Story" is a much more open and accessible word to children, and, as noted in the text, there are several reasons why you may prefer to use this word when presenting these activities to your students.** There has been much discussion in recent years of ways to combine storytelling and drama with all kinds of educational content, including science and mathematics.

Joseph Bruchac has written many excellent books and articles about Native American storytelling. Several of his books are listed in the references section. His article entitled "Storytelling and the Sacred: On the Uses of Native American Stories" (National Storytelling Journal, Spring 1987) is a summary of the deep seriousness with which these stories are viewed in Native American life, some key lessons contained in their content and telling, and the times and places considered appropriate and inappropriate for telling stories.

Among some suggestions Bruchac offers for non-Indian storytellers who tell some Native American stories are: (1) Try to learn stories not only from books but from actual experience with the ways of life and languages of living Native American peoples. When using the written text, fully research various versions. (2) When visiting with Native Americans, remember that listening and patience are cardinal virtues; do not interrupt. (3) Know what type of story you are learning. Find out when it was told, how it fits into that particular culture's world view, and if you are not certain of its origin, don't tell it. If you have heard it from a specific Native American storyteller, get permission to retell it. (4) Avoid subtly racist language or stereotypes, including words like "squaw," "papoose," or "brave," for women, children, and men. Avoid language that implies "primitive" or "ignorant" qualities. Bruchac comments that Native American cultures were often politically and culturally sophisticated, that in many tribal nations women played central leadership roles, and that Native American political organization influenced the confederation of the 13 colonies and the Constitution. In the article he recommends, *The Indian Heritage of America* by Alvin A. Josephy, Alfred A. Knopf, 1968, and there are a number of other books available on these contributions.

Evidence and Inference

The main activities in this guide can branch in many directions, and, we hope, will contain many exciting and educational experiences for your students. As their teacher, you will determine best how to adjust the activities to suit their background, level, and inclinations. Many levels of complexity are possible in undertaking the middens activity, for example, but even if the least complex approach is presented, your students will love it and learn a great deal from it.

There is absolutely no necessity with younger students to inject confusing vocabulary to describe thinking processes. The words "evidence" and "inference""need not be used. The most essential philosophy of the entire GEMS series has to do with "learning through doing," and there is plenty to *do* in this series of activities. Your students' guesses, thoughts, ideas, *inferences*, and conclusions will blossom through their hands-on involvement and creativity.

For older students, the theme of evidence leading to inference that runs throughout these activities can be a very important and conscious area of intellectual development for them. This theme is intimately related to science and mathematics, but it is also important in the social sciences, and is a central part of problem-solving and life thinking skills that are sometimes lumped under the popular heading of "common sense." Many teachers, including some in kindergarten and first grade, have remarked that after engaging in this series of activities, they can see striking growth in ways that their students analyze and evaluate physical evidence, debate possible inferences and make conclusions.

In the field of science education, it is assumed that the processes involved in making complex inferences related to science activities are best presented to students above the sixth grade level. It is said that because inferences deal with matters that are not in the "here and now," with ideas or generalizations that are more remote in terms of time or space or scale, and with things that are not experienced directly, then the cognitive development of children must be at a higher level before inference can be fully explored. Certainly inferring possibilities related to the changing of several variables requires greater cognitive development. For example, in the middens activity, older students exploring and mapping three levels might be able to conclude that the people who left the materials did not develop pottery techniques until the second time period, and that, by the third time period, clay was being used both for dishes and in jewelry.

However, we would offer two important distinctions. The first has to do with making *simple*, as opposed to complex, inferences. For example: "That piece of pottery came from a broken plate." Very young children constantly make simple inferences, sometimes accurate, sometimes not, but inferences nonetheless. We can then ask them further questions so they examine the explanations they offer, and refine them as they learn more. Your students will make many simple (and some not-so-simple!) inferences throughout this unit by offering possible explanations, based on physical evidence and their own reasoning. The more opportunities they have to practice, the more likely they are to make and refine inferences.

In addition, and as the second distinction, young children can become extremely involved in making sometimes quite complex inferences related to stories and literature. In language arts development, the process of more abstract reasoning, of wondering why a character behaves as she does, for example, certainly begins at a very early age and can become quite advanced during the elementary years. Perhaps then, the way this unit weaves the idea of making inferences and offering explanations based on evidence into language arts, as well as mathematics and science, may make it a particularly good way to introduce these important thinking processes during the early grades, regardless of the names they are given.

What is Archaeology?

Archaeologists seek to reconstruct the life and cultures of past ages through the study of objects created by people. These objects are known as *artifacts*. The study is conducted by using scientific methods to systematically uncover, recover, and make detailed investigations of evidence left behind by past cultures.

Archaeology is not simply the collection of artifacts, but, more importantly, the study of a site *to find out more about the way of life of past society*. The **systematic** process of *excavation* is one of the hallmarks of modern archaeology, even when archaeologists must complete an excavation under strict time constraints. The careful scientific nature of modern archaeology, and its primary interest in learning about the **culture** from analysis of sites, strongly distinguishes its practices from those of "pot hunters" who collect artifacts for personal financial gain. Looting of this kind has been part of recorded history since the early Egyptian kings and continues into the present. Valuable information is lost forever when grave robbers loot a burial site.

Archaeology can also be sub-divided according to whether it focuses on prehistoric societies—those that existed *before* the earliest written records—or on those that existed *after* written records were kept. The former is called Prehistorical Archaeology; the latter, Historical Archaeology. Other specialty areas include: Urban Archaeology, with excavations in urban areas; Industrial Archaeology, which focuses on the early era of the Industrial Revolution; and Underwater Archaeology. Archaeology that involves excavating items of importance very quickly before a construction project destroys or blocks the site is sometimes called "salvage archaeology."

The Archaeology Handbook by Bill McMillon, listed in the archaeology references for this unit near the back of the book, contains an excellent listing of archaeological sites in many states, Canada, and throughout the world that you can visit. Many of these sites have arrangements for volunteers to assist in excavation work. The handbook also contains a good regional listing of organizations, museums, and state agencies that specialize in archaeology, in case you may want to arrange a field trip or invite an archaeologist to make a presentation to your class or school.

Session 5:
I enjoyed session 5 five because everyone had a part and was important, it was so interesting you didn't no when or where you would find the object and you never knew what kind of object you would find. I also enjoyed getting to work as a group on such a special project.

Session 5
I liked session 5 the best because you get to act like an archeologist and find artifacts like string, beads, and rawhide. I also liked it because people got different jobs like a curator and excavator.

Bibliography and Resources

There are, of course, a huge number of books and other resources that relate to this teacher's guide. The following listings are divided into three main parts: Books for Young People on Native American Themes (with an additional brief listing for adult reference); Books that relate to other World Cultures; and Books about Archaeology and Exploring Your Own Roots.

Many teachers have their own favorite books on Native American life, and there is at least some inclusion of information about local or regional tribes in many elementary school curricula. Combining this unit with a focus on learning more about the Indigenous peoples of your region is an excellent way to extend learning and emphasize cultural diversity.

Very Special Mention

Two outstanding books by the same authors combine clearly written nature-based and science activities for children with beautiful, sensitively-told, and stirring stories, clearly identified as to tribal origin. They both are accompanied by excellent teacher's guides. These two books are highly recommended as resources of the highest quality:

Caduto, Michael J. and Bruchac, Joseph: *Keepers of the Earth: Native American Stories and Environmental Activities for Children*, Fulcrum Publishing, Golden, Colorado, 1988.

Caduto, Michael J. and Bruchac, Joseph: *Keepers of the Animals, Native American Stories and Wildlife Activities for Children*, Fulcrum Publishing, Golden, Colorado, 1991.

Books for Young People on Native American Themes

Aliki: *Corn is Maize: The Gift of the Indians*, Thomas Y. Crowell, 1976. Grades: 3–5. A story describing how corn was first cultivated, stored, and used by Native peoples of the Americas and how it came to be a main food source all over the world.

Amon, Aline: *The Earth is Sore: Native Americans on Nature*, Atheneum, New York. 1981. Grades: 4–adult. Collection of poems and songs celebrating the relationship between the earth and all creatures and mourning abuse of the environment, with information on each tribe whose views are expressed. Illustrated with black and white collage prints made from natural materials.

Baylor, Byrd: *The Desert Is Theirs*. Peter Parnall, illustrator, Charles Scribner's Sons, New York. 1975. Grades: (K–5). Lyric text describes the intimate relationship between Desert People and their land.

Baylor Byrd: *The Other Way To Listen*. Peter Parnall, illustrator, Charles Scribner's Sons, New York. 1978. Grades: K–6.

Baylor Byrd: *When Clay Sings*.Tom Bahti, illustrator, Charles Scribner's Sons, New York. 1972. Grades: 1–6. Prose poem retracing the daily life and customs of prehistoric Southwestern tribes from designs in the remains of their pottery. The striking illustrations in black, brown and ochre tones include design motifs from the Anasazi, Hohokam, Mogollon, and Mimbres cultures. In the text, parents tell their children to treat each fragment with respect because "every piece of clay is a piece of someone's life," and each has its own song. Could be related to the pottery in the middens activity.

Baylor, Byrd: *I'm In Charge of Celebrations*. Illustrated by Peter Parnall. Charles Scribner's Sons, New York. 1986. Grades: 4–9. Moving story told in the first person by a Native American girl who might seem lonely to others, but who celebrates things like a triple rainbow, a meteor shower, and a chance encounter with a coyote, delighting in her surroundings. Vivid pictures of the world of the desert.

Bierhorst, John (editor): *Lightning Inside You and Other Native American Riddles*. Illustrated by Louise Brierley. William Morrow, New York. 1992. Grades: All. Includes 140 riddles translated from twenty languages. This very stimulating book is divided into categories such as the human body, animals, things made to be used, The riddle referred to in the title comes from the Comanche people: "What is there inside you like lightning?" Answer: "Meanness."

Bruchac, Joseph and Jonathan London: *Thirteen Moons on Turtle's Back: A Native American Year of Moons*. Illustrated by Thomas Locker. Philomel Books/Putnam & Grosset, New York. 1992. Grades: 3–7. Stories from different cultures about the 13 moons believed to correspond to the scales on the shell of the turtle's back and to explain the changes in the seasons. A numbered drawing shows the location of each of the 13 moons on the shell. The names of the moons are evocative: Baby Bear Moon, Moon When Wolves Run Together, Moon of Popping Trees, Moose-Calling Moon, Wild Rice Moon.

Bruchac, Joseph: *Iroquois Stories—Heroes and Heroines, Monsters and Magic*. Illustrated by Daniel Burgevin. The Crossing Press, Freedom CA 95019. 1985. Grades 3–7. Wonderful collection of over 30 stories by a leading storyteller. Good for reading out loud to younger children and for students in third or fourth grade to read by themselves as the book is in fairly large type and written in clear, direct language.

Cohlene, Terri (adapted by): *Dancing Drum A Cherokee Legend*. Charles Reasoner, illustrator, Troll Associates, Educational Reading Services, Mahwah, New Jersey, 1990. Grades: (K–5) Retells a legend in which Dancing Drum tries to make Grandmother Sun smile on The People again. Includes a section on Cherokee history and culture.

Cohlene, Terri (adapted by): *Quillworker: A Cheyenne Legend*. Charles Reasoner, illustrator, 1990. Grades 2–5. A Cheyenne legend that explains the origins of the Big Dipper constellation. Includes information on the Cheyenne people's history and culture. Also adapted by the same author are: *Clamshell Boy: A Makah Legend*, Troll Associates, Educational Reading Services, Mahwah, New Jersey, 1990, and *Turquoise Boy: A Navajo Legend*, Troll Associates, Educational Reading Services, Mahwah, New Jersey, 1990.

de Paola, Tomie (retold and illustrated by): *The Legend of the Bluebonnet*. G.B. Putnam's Sons, New York. 1983. Grades: K–3. Set in what is now Texas, this legend tells of a young girl, She-Who-Is-Alone, whose people are desperately praying to the Great Spirits to end a drought. Only when the orphan girl sacrifices her treasured and only possession, a warrior doll with blue jay feathers, do the spirits send the rain. She is renamed One-Who-Dearly-Loved-Her-People and the bluebonnet flower comes every spring, as blue as the feathers of the blue jay.

dePaola, Tomie (retold and illustrated by): *The Legend of the Indian Paintbrush*. G.P. Putnam's Sons, New York. 1988. Grades: K–4. After a Dream Vision, the Plains Indian boy Little Gopher is inspired to paint pictures as pure as the colors in the evening sky. He gathers flowers and berries to make paints but can't capture the colors of the sunset. After another vision, he goes to a hilltop where he finds brushes filled with paint which he uses and leaves on the hill. The next day, and now every spring, the hills and meadows are ablaze with the bright color of the Indian Paintbrush.

Esbenson, Barbara J. (retold by): *Ladder to the Sky: How the Gift of Healing Came to the Ojibway Nation*. Illustrated by Helen K. Davie. Little, Brown Co., Boston. 1989. Grades: K–4. Based on a legend recorded in 1850, tells of the time when all people were healthy. When they grew old, a "shining spirit-messenger" carried them up a magic vine to the sky where they lived forever. After a grandmother climbs up the forbidden vine in pursuit of her grandson, the Great Spirit punishes the people by sending sickness and death, but then blesses them with the gift of healing. There is a very strong message here about the negative value of disobedience in the culture. The villagers call the old woman a witch and resent her for bringing "shame and disaster" to the people. Has good detail on how the Ojibway people integrated the plant world into their culture.

Esbensen, Barbara J. (retold by): *The Star Maiden*. Illustrated by Helen K. Davie. Little, Brown & Co., Boston. 1988. Grades: K–4. Based on a legend recorded in 1850 about a star who grows tired of wandering the sky and wants to live on earth. She tries becoming a rose and then a prairie flower, but finally finds her "place on earth" as a water lily.

Goble, Paul: *Buffalo Woman*. Bradbury Press, 1984. Plains Indian legend about a buffalo that turns into a girl, and the living connection between people and animals.

Goble, Paul: *Dream Wolf.* Bradbury Press/Macmillan, New York. 1990, revised edition. Originally published as The Friendly Wolf, 1974. Grades: 1–4. A Plains Indian boy and his sister wander away from a berry-picking expedition and are lost in the hills as night falls. A wolf comes to their aid, leading them back to their home. There has been close kinship with the Wolf People since then, for as long as anyone can remember. It is noted that wolves are no longer heard in the evenings at berry-picking time because they have been killed or driven away. People say that the wolves will return when we have them in our hearts and dreams again. Goble has written and illustrated many other Native American legends including the Iktomi series, humorous tales about the Trickster.

Goble, Paul: *The Girl Who Loved Wild Horses*, Bradbury Press, 1978. From the Plains Indians, the story of a girl and her love for horses.

Hoyt-Goldsmith, Diane: *Totem Pole.* Photographs by Lawrence Migdale. Holiday House, New York. 1990. Grades: 3–5. A Tsimshian Indian boy, David, describes how his father carved a totem pole for the Klallam tribe in Washington. The complete process is described and shown in color photographs, from finding a straight tree through raising the pole and holding accompanying ceremonies. Drawings show the figures of Thunderbird, Killer Whale, Bear, Raven and a Klallam Chief carved on the pole, and explain their mythic significance. The pride of the young boy in his father, dedication to the craft, and the passing on of tradition are well conveyed: "Like my father, I look for the animal shapes hidden inside the wood."

Joosse, Barbara M: *Mama, Do You Love Me?* Illustrated by Barbara Lavallee. Chronicle Books, San Francisco. 1991. Grades: K–4. This universal story of a child testing the limits of her independence is set in the Arctic. Whales, wolves, puffins, sled dogs and Inuit culture are depicted in stunning, fresh illustrations. And the answer to the child's question is always yes, even, "if you put lemmings in my mukluks." A glossary lists some animals and objects which may not be familiar (such as "ptarmigan"), noting their particular significance in the culture.

LeSueur, Meridel: *Sparrow Hawk.* illustrations by Robert Desjarlait, foreword by Vine Deloria, Jr., Holy Cow Press, 1987. A beautifully written and moving novel about a young Sauk growing to manhood and his white friend Huck, as they are caught in the midst of the Black Hawk War. The images of the closeness to the land and connection to the life-giving corn are poetic and powerful.

Lopez, Barry: *Crow and Weasel.* Illustrations by Tom Pohrt, North Point Press, San Francisco, 1990. For older students, this book chronicles the journey of two young men, Crow and Weasel, who travel farther North than any of their people have ever gone, learning lifelong lessons along the way. One of many strangers they meet is Badger, who tells them, "Remember only this one thing...the stories people tell have a way of taking care of them. If stories come to you, care for them. And learn to give them away where they are needed. Sometimes a person needs a story more than food to stay alive. That is why we put these stories in each other's memory. This is how people care for themselves."

Mayo, Gretchen W: *Earthmaker's Tales: North American Indian Stories about Earth Happenings*. Walker and Co., New York. 1989. Grades: 5–7. This is a particularly appropriate book for this unit, providing many specific examples of myths or stories that explain natural events (the same thing students do in the "Myths" sessions of the GEMS guide). Among the natural events that the stories relate to are: earthquakes, floods, night and day, storms, thunder and lightning, fog, and volcanoes. A teacher could choose two or three of her favorites to widen student acquaintance with different cultures and/or orient them to their task.

Mayo, Gretchen Will: *Star Tales: North American Indian Stories about the Stars*. Beautifully illustrated collection of stories about moon, stars, and nighttime sky.

McDermott, Gerald: *Arrow to the Sun*. The Viking Press, Inc., New York. 1974. Grades: K–3. An adaptation of the Pueblo Indian myth that explains how the spirit of the Lord of the Sun was brought to the world. After passing through the trial of the Kiva of Lightning on a quest for his father, the boy is transformed and is filled with the power of the Sun.

O'Dell, Scott: *Sing Down the Moon*. Houghton Mifflin Co., Boston. 1970. Dell Publishing, New York. 1976. Grades: 6–12. Told through the eyes of 14-year-old Bright Morning, a Navajo girl who lives in Canyon de Chelly, Arizona in 1863. We see the uprooting of her people's life, first by Spanish slavers, then by U.S. soldiers who force them to go on a 300-mile Long Walk to Fort Sumner. The major events are tragic and cruel. Bright Morning does survive to return to her home. Accounts of daily life include construction of shelters, preparations for the marriage and Womanhood ceremonies, making garments, planting seed, and the logistics of travel.

Ortiz, Simon: *The People Shall Continue*. Illustrated by Sharol Graves. Children's Book Press, San Francisco, 1977. A poetic and powerful book by a fine Acoma poet that can serve as an excellent introduction for even very young students to Native American peoples and issues. Particularly strong in its emphasis on the continuing stream of resistance to domination.

Polacco, Patricia: *Boat Ride With Lillian Two Blossom*. Philomel/Putnam & Grosset, New York. 1988. Grades: K–4. A wise and mysterious Native American woman takes William and Mabel on a boat ride, starting in Michigan and ranging through the sky. Explanations for the rain, the wind, and the changing nature of the sky refer to spirits such as the caribou or polar bear, which are magically shown.

The Native Americans: An Illustrated History
Turner Publishing Company, Atlanta, Georgia, 1993.

An excellent book on Native American culture, tradition, and present-day struggles, with original art, photographs, and clear text. This beautifully-illustrated book has sections authored by David Hurst Thomas, Jay Miller, Richard White, Peter Nabokov, Philip J. Deloria, and an introduction by Alvin D. Josephy, Jr.

Rodanas, Kristina: *Dragonfly's Tale*. Clarion Books/Houghton Mifflin Co., New York. 1991. Grades: K–4. Based on a Zuni legend, this story tells of the origin of the dragonfly with an underlying theme of appreciating one's blessings. After the people foolishly waste food in a festive "food fight," the Corn Maidens teach them a lesson by sending a famine and drought. A little boy fashions a toy insect from a cornstalk for his sister. The toy comes to life, secures the help of the Corn Maidens in providing a harvest, and can be seen every summer humming among the corn as a dragonfly. The illustrations depict the landscape, honeycombed lodgings, and ceremonial and daily clothing particular to the culture with great warmth and detail.

Shemie, Bonnie: *Native Dwellings* (series). Tundra Books, Montreal, Quebec, Canada. From Tundra Books of Northern New York, P.O. Box 1030, Plattsburgh, NY 12901. 1991. Houses of Hide and Earth (Plains), Houses of Bark (Woodland), and Houses of Snow, Skin and Bones (Northern) deal with the structure of Native American dwellings, including the building materials, the techniques and tools, and how they were/are lived in. The books are designed with a number of double-paged spreads showing a panoramic view and with smaller insets showing details such as tools. The new Houses of Wood, on Northwest Coast dwellings, has especially effective artwork. The next volume scheduled in the series is Houses of Straw and Mud about Southeastern Indian buildings.

Sneve, Virginia Driving Hawk (editor): *Dancing Teepees: Poems of American Indian Youth*. Stephen Gammell, illustrator, Holiday House. New York. 1989. Grades: 3–8. A selection of chants, lullabies, prayers, and poems from the Native American oral tradition. These celebrate rites of passage and other symbolic events such as a buffalo hunt or corn ceremony. The muted color illustrations of beadwork, petroglyphs, and motifs derived from nature are beautiful and well matched to the verses.

Steptoe, John: *The Story of Jumping Mouse*. Lothrop, Lee & Shepard, New York. 1984. Grades: 3–6. In this retelling of a Native American legend, the smallest and humblest of creatures (a mouse) becomes the noblest (the eagle). In a spirit of hope, compassion, and generosity, the young mouse gives away his sense of sight and smell to other needy animals but is rewarded by his transformation. Beautiful wash drawings capture the world of forest and desert from a low-on-the-ground perspective.

Trimble, Stephen: *The Village of Blue Stone*. Illustrated by Jennifer Dewey and Deborah Reade. Macmillan, New York. 1990. Grades: 5–8. Recreates one year in the life of an imaginary Anasazi pueblo in 1100 A.D. in what is now New Mexico. Fictional characters such as Badger Claws (the Sun Watcher), Turquoise Boy, Dragonfly, and baby Blue Feather are involved in the full range of events of daily life including pottery–making, a wedding, the Harvest Dance, and illness and a death. Illustrates the connections between the land and architecture, work and art, material culture and spiritual beliefs.

Yue, Charlotte and David: *The Tipi: A Center of Native American Life*. Alfred A. Knopf, New York. 1984. Grades: 5–8. This book describes not only the structure and uses of tipis, but the Plains social and cultural context as well. There are good charts, exact measurements, and information on the advantages of the cone shape. The central role played by women in constructing the tipi and in owning it are discussed. While this book includes some mention of the negative consequences of European conquest, noting that in some places tipis were outlawed, it is much weaker in this important area, and should be supplemented with other books.

Van Laan, Nancy: *Rainbow Crow: A Lenape Tale*. Illustrated by Beatriz Vidal. Alfred A. Knopf, New York. 1989. Grades: K–3. Retelling of the legend of Rainbow Crow (also known as Raven) as heard at a ceremony in Pennsylvania. When the weather brings a long period of snow, the animals become worried and decide to send a messenger to the Great Sky Spirit. The most beautiful bird, brightly colored Rainbow Crow, offers to make the long journey and is rewarded with the gift of fire which he carries in his beak. Forever after, he has a hoarse cry and blackened feathers, but with tiny rainbows of color. The illustrations are perfectly wedded to the text.

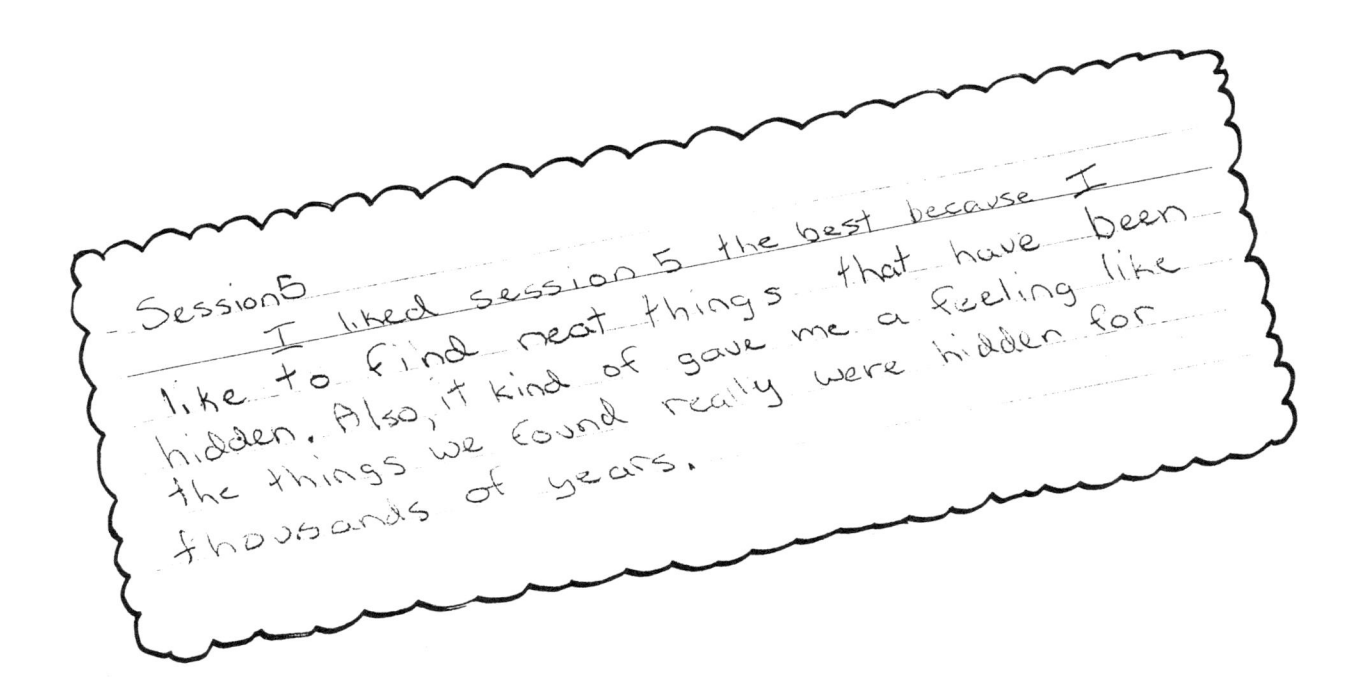

Session 5
I liked session 5 the best because I like to find neat things that have been hidden. Also, it kind of gave me a feeling like the things we found really were hidden for thousands of years.

Teacher Suggestions and Audiovisual Resources

We received numerous reference suggestions from teachers who tested these activities in classrooms across the country, many of which appear on the previous list. Among others that teachers suggested are: many other books by Paul Goble; *Native American Folk Tales* by Joe Hayes; *American Indian Poetry,* selected by Helen Addison Howard; *White Deer, Ceremony in the Circle of Life* by Robert San Souci, also *Legend of Scarface* and *Song of Sedna* by the same author; *How Rabbit Stole the Fire and Who Will Be the Sun?* by Joanna Troughton; *Masks and Mask Makers* by Kari Hunt and Bernice Wells Carson; and, for teacher reference, *The Power of Myth,* by Joseph Campbell.

A teacher from the San Francisco Bay Area suggested a video on "Ohlone culture" that is available through the East Bay Regional Parks, at (510) 635-0135. There are many other excellent film and video resources. Contact a library or resource center in your area. The resource and reference listings in the Caduto and Bruchac books noted above and the "Rethinking Columbus" resource listed under "Adult Reference" materials below are wide-ranging and excellent. Here are several other sources of materials:

American Indian Library Association, 207 Hillman Library, University of Pittsburgh, Pittsburg, Pennseylvania 15260, (412) 648-7723 has bibliographies and programs.

American Indian Program, 300 Caldwell Hall, Cornell University, Ithaca, New York, 14853, (607) 255-6587, has program guides and curriculum packages for teachers on Native Americans.

Canyon Record and Indian Arts. 4143 N. 16th St., Phoenix, AZ 85016. (602) 266-4823 is a major distributor of American Indian-related audiotapes, records, and CDs.

HONOR, Inc. at 2647 N. Stowell Ave., Milwaukee, WI 53211, (414) 963-1324, carries a number of resources, focusing on treaty rights, and including "More Bows Than Arrows," a classic film to increase understanding of Native Americans that can be rented as a video. Also available is "Treaties, Truth, and Trust," presenting answers from Wisconsin tribal leaders to commonly asked questions on treaty rights.

National Geographic Society, Educational Services, Department 82, Washington, D.C. 20036, (301) 948-5926 carries a map entitled "Indians of North America," an archaeological and enthnological map, with notes, 1979.

Native Americans on Film and Video (Volume II, 1988) includes detailed descriptions of about 400 films and videos about Indians and the Inuit of the Americas. This catalog is available from the National Museum of the American Indian, Broadway at 155th St.. New York, NY 10032. (212) 283-2420.

Audiotapes

Ross, Gayle: *How Rabbit Tricked Otter and Other Cherokee Animal Stories*, Audiotape, Caedmon, an imprint of Harper Audio, HarperCollins Publishers, Inc., New York, 1991. This is a wonderful collection of stories told by a nationally known storyteller who is also the great-great-great granddaughter of John Ross, who was the Principal Chief of the Cherokee nation during the infamous "Trail of Tears."

Storytelling Catalog from National Association for the Preservation and Perpetuation of Storytelling (NAPPS), Box 309, Jonesborough, Tennessee 37659. This publication lists tapes, records, films, and videos of stories told by storytellers. This organization holds an annual national festival and sponsors regional festivals as well.

Sources for Native American Myths Resource Page

1. *Rainbow Crow* , retold by Nancy Van Laan, illustrated by Beatriz Vidal, Dragonfly Books, Alfred A. Knopf, New York, 1989.

2. *Indian Masks and Myths of the West* by Joseph H. Wherry, Bonanza Books, New York, 1969.

3. and 4. *California Indian Nights* by Edward W. Gifford and Gwendoline Harris Block, University of London Press, 1990, Lincoln and London. Originally published in 1930.

5. *They Dance in the Sky, Native American Star Myths* by Jean Guard Monroe and Ray A. Williamson, Houghton Mifflin, Boston, 1987.

Sources for World Culture Myths Resource Page

1. *Ancient Cosmologies* by Carmen Blacker and Michael Loewe, London, George Allen and Unwin, Ltd., 1975

2. *Moon Was Tired of Walking on Air* by Natalia M. Belting, illustrated by Will Hillenbrand, Houghton Mifflin Co., Boston, 1992

3. *Legends of the Sun and Moon* by Eric and Tessa Hadley, illustrated by Jan Nesbitt, Cambridge University Press, Cambridge, 1983.

4. *The Truth About the Moon* by Clayton Bess, illustrated by Rosekrans Hoffman, Houghton Mifflin Co., Boston, 1983.

5. *Land of the Long White Cloud* by Kiri Te Kanawa, illustrated by Michael Foreman, Arcade Publishing, New York, Little, Brown and Co., 1989.

A Few Adult Reference Materials on Native American Issues

Bigelow, Bill; Miner, Barbara; Peterson, Bob: *Rethinking Columbus: Teaching About the 500th Anniversary of Columbus's Arrival in America,* a special issue of Rethinking Schools, available from Rethinking Schools, 1001 Keefe Avenue, Milwaukee, Wisconsin, 53212, (414) 964-9646. This is a concise and wide-ranging series of articles, teaching and curriculum suggestions, and information for teachers on the Quincentennial. It includes a survey of the portrayals of Columbus in children's literature entitled "Once Upon a Genocide," poetry, an extensive resource list and bibliography, student contributions, and many illustrations.

Crosby, Alfred W. Jr.: *The Columbian Exchange.* Greenwood Press, Westport, Connecticut, 1972.

Deloria, Vine Jr. *Custer Died for Your Sins.* MacMillan, New York, 1969; *God Is Red.* Grosset and Dunlap, New York, 1973; *Behind the Trail of Broken Treaties: An Indian Declaration of Independence.* Delacorte Press, New York, 1974.

Josephy, Alvin: *The Indian Heritage of America,* Alfred A. Knopf, New York, 1968.

Mander, Jerry: *In the Absence of the Sacred: The Failure of Technology and the Rise of the Indian Nations,* Sierra Club Books, 1991.

McLain, Gary: *The Indian Way,* John Muir Publishing, Santa Fe, New Mexico, 1990.

Nabokov, Peter, editor: *Native American Testimony: An Anthology of Indian and White Relations, First Encounter to Dispossession.* Thomas Y. Crowell, New York, 1978. An outstanding collection of short documents providing eloquent historical and human drama to the interaction between Native Americans and European settlers over hundreds of years. This is an excellent and moving book for students to read, from early prophecies before 1492 to Black Elk's plea to the Six Powers of the World: "Hear me in my sorrow, for I may never call again. O make my people live."

Pearce, Roy Harvey: *Savigism and Civilization: A Study of the Indian and American Mind.* University of California Press, Los Angeles, 1988.

Sale, Kirkpatrick: *The Conquest of Paradise: Christopher Columbus and the Columbian Legacy,* Alfred A. Knopf, New York, 1990. Particularly pertinent for study of the Columbus Quincentennial.

Slapin, Beverly; Seale, Doris: *Books Without Bias: Through Indian Eyes,* New Society Publishers, Philadelphia, Pennsylvania, 3rd edition, 1990. Includes excellent articles, reviews of children's books about Native Americans, and a checklist designed to detect stereotyping and other negative images that appear in some children's (and adult) literature.

Waldman, Carl: *Atlas of the North American Indian*, maps and illustrations by Molly Braun, Facts on File Publications, New York, 1985. An excellent and detailed survey of the Native peoples throughout North America, their histories, and original homelands, with extraordinary maps, and carefully written text.

Weatherford, Jack: *Indian Givers: How the Indians of the Americas Transformed the World*, Ballantine Books, 1988. Native Roots: How the Indians Enriched America, Crown Publishers, Inc., New York, 1991.

A Mystery Extension

Hillerman, Tony: *Dance Hall of the Dead*, Harper & Row, New York, 1973. An outstanding mystery with much information on Native American spirituality in the Southwest. Focuses on the Zuni and Navajo, and an archaeological excavation in their midst. Investigative logic is intricately interwoven with Native wisdom, and (connecting with this unit) archaeology figures prominently in the plot. (We can't tell you anymore!) If you are adapting this unit upward for junior high or high school students, this book would be an excellent accompaniment. The author has written a number of other similar mysteries.

World Cultures

Aardema, Vern: *Why Mosquitoes Buzz in People's Ears*, Leo and Diane Dillon, illustrators, Dial Books for Young Readers, New York, 1975. Grades: K–6. This retold West African folktale is a great accompaniment to student explanations created during the "Myths" activity.

Bess, Clayton: *The Truth About the Moon*. Illustrated by Rosekrans Hoffman. Houghton Mifflin Co., Boston. 1983. Grades: K–4. An African boy named Sumu is puzzled by the changing size of the moon and asks for an explanation. His father says there is only one moon and that the moon he saw last night is the same moon he will see tomorrow. "It is growing, just as a child like you grows to be a man like me. It starts small, just a silver sliver, and every night grows bigger and bigger until it is as big as it can be, a full circle. Then, just as a man grows smaller when he is very old, so does the moon. Smaller and smaller until death." His mother explains that there is only one moon. "It is like a woman. And you know how sometimes a woman will grow larger and larger, more and more round?" The Chief tells a long tale about the sun and the moon being married and how the moon lost its heat. Wonderful examples of how stories can "explain" natural phenomena.

Blia Xiong (told by), Spagnoli, Cathy (adapted by): *Nine-in-One Grrr! Grrr!* Illustrated by Nancy Hom. Children's Book Press, San Francisco. 1989. Grades: K–3. This folktale from Laos explains why there are not too many tigers on the Earth. When the first female tiger asks the kind and gentle God Shao how many cubs she will have, he tells her she will have nine cubs a year, if she remembers his words. Tiger does not have a great memory, so she makes up a little song to remember: "Nine-in-One, Grr! Grr!" When the other animals find this out, they are worried because that many tigers could eat all of them. A clever bird succeeds in distracting the tiger long enough to make her forget the song, then convinces her that the song was, "One-in-Nine, Grr! Grr!" (one cub every nine years). And, "that is why, the Hmong people say, we don't have too many tigers on earth today." This story is a compelling explanatory myth, and could open a discussion of the balance of nature. Importantly, the story also helps represent the culture of a people who have been among the large numbers of recent Asian immigrants to the United States.

Bowden, Joan C.: *Why the Tides Ebb and Flow*. Illustrated by Marc Brown. Houghton Mifflin Co., Boston. 1979. Grades: K–4. A feisty old woman bargains with the Sky Spirit, finally gaining a hut, a daughter and son-in-law, and the loan of a very special rock to beautify her yard. The fact that she borrows the rock twice each day from a hole in the bottom of the sea explains why the tides ebb and flow. The tale is not attributed to any specific culture, but the design motifs seem inspired by Africa.

Byrd Baylor: *The Way To Start A Day*, Peter Parnall, illustrator, Macmillan Publishing Company, New York. 1977. Grades: K–3. Gives examples, with beautiful illustrations, of the variety of ways that different peoples around the world celebrate the dawn from drum beats to gifts of gold. Caldecott Honor Book.

Cole, Judith: *The Moon, the Sun, and the Coyote*. Illustrated by Cecile Schoberle. Simon & Schuster, New York. 1991. Grades: K–4. The moon and the sun quarrel over whether the animals of the day or the night are the most beautiful. The coyote is the moon's favorite and she grants him a number of wishes that result in one change too many in his appearance. He still sings to the moon at night trying to get more attention. This is not a traditional tale, but original to the author. The illustrations do not reflect a specific culture, but seem to be inspired by Latin or South American design motifs.

Dayrell, Elphinstone: *Why the Sun and the Moon Live in the Sky*. Illustrated by Blair Lent. Houghton Mifflin Co., Boston. 1968. Grades: K–4. Dayrell's adaptation of a Nigerian folktale explaining the origin of the world was first published in 1910. The sun and his wife, the moon, built a large house for entertaining the water. By the time the water and all his people have flowed in and over the top of the roof, the sun and moon are forced to go up into the sky. The main characters and the fish and water animals are all represented as African people in tribal clothing and masks in brown, green, blue and gold-patterned drawings. Caldecott Honor book.

Flournoy, Valerie: *The Patchwork Quilt*. Illustrated by Jerry Pinkney. Dial/Dutton, New York. 1985. Grades: K–5. Tanya, an African-American child, and her grandmother make a quilt using scraps cut from the family's old clothing including her African princess Halloween costume. The grandmother becomes ill and the whole family becomes involved in completing the quilt of memories. Referring to this "masterpiece," the grandmother says, "A quilt won't forget. It can tell your life story."

Gerson, Mary-Joan (retold by): *Why the Sky Is Far Away*. Illustrated by Hope Meryman. Harcourt Brace Jovanovich, San Diego. 1974. Grades: K–4. Nigerian folktale about the sky that also offers a strong moral message against squandering natural resources. It tells of a time when the sky was so close to the earth that anyone who was hungry just cut off a piece of sky and ate it. The king even had a special team of servants whose only job was to cut and shape the sky for ordinary meals and special ceremonies. But the sky was getting tired of being wasted. When one woman throws away a leftover piece saying "what does it matter? ... one more piece on the rubbish heap," the sky finally moves away. Ever since then people have had to work very hard to grow their own food.

Gutierrez, Douglas and Maria F. Oliver: *The Night of the Stars*. Kane/Miller Book Publishers, P.O. Box 529, Brooklyn, NY.11231-0005. 1988. Also available in Spanish. Grades: 3–5. The story of a man long ago who did not like the night and dark sky. One night he climbs the highest mountain, and, on his tiptoes, pokes a hole in the black sky, so a pinprick of light shines through. Then he pokes many more, and one really big one creates the moon. That night no one slept—everyone stays up late admiring the moon and stars. Nice connection to the "How the Stars Came to Be" story in Session 4.

Hamilton, Virginia, *In the Beginning: Creation Stories from Around the World*. Barry Moser, illustrator. Harcourt, Brace Jovanovich, Publishers, San Diego, New York, London, 1988. Grades: All. An illustrated collection of twenty-five legends explaining the creation of the world, including several of Native American origin, with commentary placing the myth geographically and by type of myth, such as, "world parent," "creation from nothing," and "separation of earth and sky." Some of the selections are extracted from larger works such as the Popol Vuh of the Mayan people or the Icelandic Edda. Newbery Honor Book.

Hamilton, Virginia: *The All Jahdu Storybook*. Illustrated by Barry Moser. Harcourt Brace Jovanovich, San Diego. 1991. Grades: K–6. Collection of stories about the trickster, Jahdu. They hinge on no single tradition, but aim to express the timelessness and worldwide relevance of folklore. The diverse illustrations reflect the changes in Jahdu. One minute he is in the jungle, the next in a taxi in Harlem. Characters he meets may be animals like Bandicoot Rat or the chicken Cackle G., or Shadow, Thunder, or Grass.

Kanawa, Kiri Te: *Land of the Long White Cloud: Maori Myths, Tales, and Legends*. Illustrated by Michael Foreman. Arcade Publishing/Little, Brown, Boston. 1989. Originally published in Great Britain by Pavilion Books. Grades: K–5. Collection of stories of the Indigenous people of New Zealand about Maui, a trickster and mischief maker; the *woman* in the moon, the birds, the lakes, rivers and trees, and assorted fairies and monsters. The tales are interspersed with commentary by the author, a well-known opera star who is of Maori and Irish heritage. The very exciting tales reflect the life of a people whose survival depended on their close knowledge of the sea in all its changes.

Lee, Jeanne M. (retold and illustrated by): *Legend of the Milky Way*. Henry Holt & Co., New York. 1982. Grades: K–5. Retells the legend of the weaver Princess who came down from heaven to marry a mortal; her mother punishes them by making them into stars separated by the Silver River (the Milky Way). A note at the end of the book adds that the Chinese celebrate this story on the seventh day of the seventh Chinese month. If it rains that night, they say the princess is crying because she must say goodbye to her husband. The last page explains which familiar stars and constellations represent the characters in this legend.

Lester, Julius: *How Many Spots Does a Leopard Have? and other Tales*. David Shannon, illustrator. Scholastic, Inc., New York. 1989. Grades 6–10. A fine collection of African folktales, including two Jewish tales and an African-Jewish one. Written for somewhat older students, some of these stories could be read out loud to younger students. We learn why the sun and moon live in the sky, why monkeys live in trees, and why dogs chase cats, but no one ever finds out how many spots the leopard really has!

Mollel, Tololwa M.: *A Promise to the Sun*. Illustrated by Beatriz Vidal. Joy Street Books/Little, Brown and Co., Boston. 1992. Grades: K–4. This African tale explains why bats fly only at night. In a time of great drought, the birds draw lots to see who will journey to seek rain, and the lot falls to a visiting bat. The bat successfully persuades the Sun to bring about rain, but is left holding the bag when the birds don't follow through on a promise to the Sun. To avoid the Sun's wrath, the bat hides in a cave and lives there to this day.

Moroney, Lynn (adapted by): *Elinda Who Danced in the Sky*. Illustrated by Veg Reisberg. Children's Book Press, San Francisco. 1990. Grades: K–4. Estonian folk tale about the sky goddess Elinda who overcomes her disappointment at losing Prince Borealis whose land would not let him leave. There are clever explanations of why Elinda turned down previous suitors—the North Star is distant and unmoving, the Moon always takes the same narrow path, and the Sun's light is too harsh and overpowering. She returns to her vocation of guiding the birds in their migrations. Her wedding veil, woven from dewdrops and dragonfly wings, remains as the Milky Way.

Musgrave, Margaret: *Ashanti to Zulu, African Tradition*, Leo and Diane Dillon, illustrators, Dial Books, New York, 1976. Grades: 3–7. Beautifully illustrated and well researched alphabet book that describes African ceremonies, celebrations, and day-to day customs and reflects the richness and diversity of the peoples and cultures. In most of the paintings, a man, woman, child, an artifact, a local animal, and the living quarters are shown so that each page is quite detailed, even though all these elements might not ordinarily be seen together. A note indicates that the border design is based on the Kano Knot, a 17th-century design that symbolizes endless searching.

Polacco, Patricia: *The Keeping Quilt*. Simon & Schuster, New York. 1988. Grades: K–5. A homemade quilt ties together the lives of four generations of an immigrant Jewish family. Made from their old clothes, it helps them remember back home "like having the family in Russia dance around us at night." The quilt is shown being used in marriage ceremonies, as a tablecloth, and as a blanket for a newborn child, symbolizing the family's enduring love and faith.

Vautier, Ghislaine: *The Shining Stars: Greek Legends of the Zodiac* . Adapted by Kenneth McLeish. Cambridge University Press, New York, 1981. Grades: K–6. Greek legends ("space fiction about the stars") connected to each of the twelve star-signs. Includes information about stars and star–maps.

Wilson, Barbara K.: *The Turtle and the Island: A Folktale from Papua New Guinea*. Illustrated by Frane Lessac. J.B. Lippincott, New York. 1990. Originally published in Great Britain by Frances Lincoln Limited, 1990. Grades: K–4. Retelling of a New Guinea creation legend that the island was made by a great sea turtle, the mother of all sea turtles. The turtle makes the island by adding more sand and rocks to a high hill. Then she brings the lonely sole man in the ocean from his cave to the island together with a lonely weeping woman. They have beautiful children whose children have more children. The vibrant illustrations show the lovable sea turtle and an island teeming with plant and marine life.

Winter, Jeanette: *Diego*. Alfred A. Knopf, New York. 1991. Grades: K–4. Story of the great Mexican muralist Diego Rivera with special attention to his childhood and how it influenced his art. Important themes here are the relationship between art and society and the primacy of direct experience for an artist. Good connection to the art of this unit's "Masks" activities.

Yarbrough, Camille: *Cornrows*. Illustrated by Carole Byard. Coward, McCann Inc., New York. 1979. Grades: K–5. This powerful and tender book recounts a family story that Mama and Great-Grammaw tell as they braid intricate cornrow patterns in the childrens' hair. This book blends musically poetic accounts of proud African traditions, brutal slavery, cultural bedrock and beauty, with the achievements of many famous African-Americans, and a strong, loving sense of family. It could be read as part of this unit to introduce African-American contributions in general, and more specifically, to discuss the way the braiding of cornrows, the telling of stories, and the depiction of masks and sculptures connects to the unit and to modern childrens' understanding of their own cultures.

Yen, Clara (retold by): *Why Rat Comes First: A Story of the Chinese Zodiac*. Illustrated by Hideo C. Yoshida. Children's Book Press, San Francisco. 1991. Grades: K–4.This version of a tale explaining the order of the animals in the Chinese cycle of years was created by the author's father. The Jade King invites all the animals to a feast, but only 12 show up. He rewards them by naming a year after each animal, starting with the rat whose quick thinking wins him first place. More fun comes after the story is done, when each person can look up her/his birth year and the corresponding animal and characteristics. This book could also be used to discuss the lunar calendar, and the different ways that world cultures keep track of time.

Archaeology and Exploring Your Own Roots

Barker, Philip: *Understanding Archaeological Excavation*, St. Martin's Press, New York, 1986.

Cooper, Kay: *Who Put the Cannon in the Courthouse Square: A Guide to Uncovering the Past*. Illustrated by Anthony Accardo. Walker and Co., New York. 1985. Grades: 5–adult. Focuses on researching local history, not only people, but also landmarks, battles, accidents and natural disasters, cemeteries, and other secret places. Chapters on doing research at libraries, museums, and interviewing individual resources. An appendix includes a summary of three secondary school local history projects.

Dunrea, Oliver: *Skara Brae: The Story of a Prehistoric Village*, Holiday House. 1985. Grades: 4–8. This book describes a stone age settlement preserved almost intact in the sand dunes of one of the Orkney Islands, how it came to be discovered in the mid-nineteenth century, and what it reveals about life and culture of this prehistoric community. Learning about the archaeological aspects of this discovery sheds light on the techniques practiced in the middens activity.

Hilton, Suzanne: *Who Do You Think You Are?: Digging for Your Family Roots*. Westminster Press, Philadelphia. 1976. Grades: 6–adult. Describes how to do primary and secondary research, to construct a family tree, and to find "problem" records for immigrants, adopted children, Native Americans or African slave ancestors, with the example of Alex Haley and his research for the historic "Roots" TV series. The author advocates looking at history in a new way, as made by one's own people.

Macauley, David: *Motel of the Mysteries*. Houghton Mifflin Co., Boston. 1979. Grades: 6–adult. Cleverly illustrated archaeological satire in which fragments of the lost civilization of "Usa" are excavated including a supposed tomb, Room #26 at the Motel of the Mysteries, protected by a sacred seal ("Do Not Disturb" sign). For older students, this book could be a particularly apt accompaniment to the activities in the GEMS unit, in that it features an elaborate and logically-constructed train of inferences based on partial evidence. Reading this book, whose conclusions they know to be askew, can encourage students to maintain a healthy and irreverent skepticism about their own and others' inferences and conclusions, providing insight into the intricacies and pitfalls of the reasoning processes involved.

LIFE magazine (the editors of): *Early Man*, Life Nature Library, Time Inc., 1965.

Mazonowicz, Douglas: *Voices from the Stone Age*, Gallery of Prehistoric Paintings, 1974.

Merriman, Nick: *Early Humans*, Eye Witness Books, Alfred A. Knopf, New York, 1989.

McMillon, Bill: *The Archaeology Handbook, A Fieldbook and Research Guide*, John Wiley & Sons, Inc., 1991. An excellent and very clearly written book that explains what archaeologists do, provides concise and well illustrated examples of numerous techniques, and includes an extensive list of "what's, where's and how-to's" throughout the United States and the world, including sites, excavations, field schools, parks, museums, and specialized travel agencies. The sections on preparing and excavating a site may be particularly useful in planning and/or providing background for the middens activity.

Oleksy, Walter G: *Treasures of the Land, Messner*, New York, 1981.

Stein, Sara: *The Evolution Book*, Workman Publishing, New York, 1986.

Williams, Barbara: *Mitzi and Frederick the Great*, Emily Arnold McCully, illustrator, E.P. Dutton, New York, 1984. Grades 5–9. Mitzi spends a summer with her archaeologist mother and her brother (Frederick) on a dig in Chaco Canyon, a Native American historical site in the Southwest known for its great architectural sophistication. In addition to lively family dynamics, the story includes accurate information on archaeology and its techniques.

Wilson, Josleen: *The Passionate Amateur's Guide to Archaeology in the United States*, Collier Books, New York, 1980.

Weitzman, David: *My Backyard History Book*. Illustrated by James Robertson. Little, Brown and Co., Boston. 1975. Grades: 4–12. A do-it-yourself history primer with activities and projects for tracing your own roots. Create a birthday time capsule, be creative with family photographs using a photocopy machine, make a family map, record family activities and memories through photography, oral history, or gravestone rubbings. Emphasizes the theme that the past lies all around us and history is more than just dates.

Wolfman, Ira: *Do People Grow on Family Trees?: Genealogy for Kids and Other Beginners*. Illustrated by Michael Klein. Workman Publishing Co., New York. 1991. Grades: 5–12. The author was inspired to compile this guide by trying to research his four grandparents who all emigrated through Ellis Island. How to be an "Ancestor Detector," including tracing family records and finding documents, and general background material on American immigration and family names. With many photographs and short display articles, this book captures the reader's attention.

Enterprise for Education, 1320A Santa Monica Mall, Santa Monica, California 90401, has available a booklet called Hazardous Wastes from Homes with a woman archaeologist on the cover, and numerous short features on waste, garbage, and how human beings in earlier times managed waste, with a strong focus on the critical issues of hazardous waste that face society today.

Summary Outlines

Session 1: Natural Collecting and Sorting

Getting Ready

1. Take a walk to check out a route for a neighborhood walk.

2. Gather 5 to 10 samples of natural and non-natural objects.

Introducting Natural Objects

1. Tell the class they'll be taking a walk. Ask for predictions about natural and non-natural objects they may find.

2. Show the objects you collected. Using two yarn loops for natural and non-natural categories, have students help you place objects in the loops and explain their reasoning.

Introducing the Walk

1. Discuss guidelines: collect only natural, non-living objects; only from the ground; collect multiples of one object, as well as diverse objects.

2. Divide class into groups of four. Explain that the group will share the objects found, will have about 15 minutes, and should fill bag one-third to one-half full.

3. Students may also collect litter and place it in a class litter bag the teacher carries.

4. Give a bag to each group and take students on the walk.

Free Exploration of the Collections

1. Gather the class and ask for brief descriptions of what they found.

2. Have each group carefully empty contents of their bag onto a piece of newspaper.

3. Allow plenty of time for free exploration.

Sorting the Collections

1. Ask students to sort their objects into two piles, or categories.

2. They can sort any way they agree upon; there are no "right" or "wrong" ways.

3. Give each team two yarn loops. They can create a third "outside the loop" category if they wish.

4. Circulate as students sort. Allow time for each group to do at least one sort.

5. Have groups report on how they sorted and create ongoing list of categories on board.

6. As time permits, challenge student to sort a different way (s).

"Secret Sort"

1. Introduce the game: a group sorts in one way, but instead of reporting about it, quietly thinks of a word to describe the category or kind of sort, and writes that word on a card, placed face down.

2. Hand out index cards and pencils.

3. After groups have labelled their sort, explain that each group will move clockwise to the next table to try to guess the "secret sort" of that group, then look at the card. As time permits, keep rotating the groups.

4. Ask students to report new categories they created and add to list.

Evaluating Evidence

1. Ask students what they can say about the neighborhood, based on what they collected.

2. Encourage students to distinguish between observations and inferences.

Session 2: Making Masks and Inferences

Getting Ready

Gather newspaper, card stock, glue, scissors, and the bags of objects students collected.

Introducing the Masks

1. Explain that many tribes and nations of Native Americans and peoples all over the world have used all kinds of objects from their environment to make masks.

2. They will each make their own mask, using the piece of cardboard/paper plate as a base and gluing on the natural objects.

3. Encourage student creativity. Establish rules for sharing as needed, including suggestions from students. Set a time limit for completing work.

4. Distribute the materials. Have students write their names on the back of the cardboard and begin making their masks.

Making the Masks

1. Circulate, asking questions to encourage creativity.

2. Have related activities available for students who finish early.

3. After masks are completed, have students clean up their work areas, saving unused materials for future activities and placing masks in a central display area to dry.

Sharing, Sorting, and Guessing Masks

1. Gather students to look at all the masks carefully. Ask for their observations. How are they different? Similar?

2. Challenge students to "graph" the masks by attributes.

3. Conduct a mask guessing game by describing one and challenging students to identify it. Then volunteers can do the same while other students guess.

Making Inferences Based on Masks

1. Remind students of the earlier class discussion when they made inferences about their neighborhood, based on their collections.

2. Explain that this kind of reasoning process is what anthropologists use when studying objects, including masks from ancient cultures.

3. Ask students to imagine their masks are part of a museum collection and to act as anthropologists as they look at each mask, asking questions like: what might it have been used for? What can you tell about the people and the environment? What about the mask makes you think that?

4. Discuss similarities and differences of the masks, and focus on why it might be important to learn about diverse ways of doing things.

Session 3: Creating Myths

Getting Ready

1. Decide which and how many of the five pictures you want to display.

2. Mount the pictures with captions as appropriate.

3. Decide whether you want to have the masks handy.

4. Assign partners as appropriate.

Setting the Stage

1. Ask the students to imagine themselves where they are now, 2000 years ago, and discuss their ideas about how things would be then.

2. List their ideas about things they would have seen then.

3. Explain that Native Americans of long ago were careful observers of the world around them. They told stories, or myths, that were passed on over generations. Different tribes and nations had differing cultures and myths/stories. These stories often sought to explain or reflect things in nature that people saw and wondered about.

4. Tell the class the two short stories summarized from stories of the Modoc and Pomo peoples of California.

5. Depending on your class, you may want to give other examples, or model making up a story as a group. If not, put up the five pictures of natural phenomena.

Explaining Observations Through Stories

1. Ask your students to imagine themselves observing these phenomena 2000 years ago.

2. Explain the challenge: to work with a partner to create a story together that explains how something came to be the way it is.

3. Have students first choose one of the pictures to explain with a story. They do not necessarily need to write down the stories. They first discuss the story together, then make a drawing to illustrate it.

4. Distribute paper, pencils and crayons (or markers) and focus the class on the challenge.

The Activity: Students Create Myths

1. Circulate as student pairs work, giving encouragement.

2. Remind students to draw large pictures, labelled if possible. Collect the drawings and written stories, if they did write them down, for sharing in the next session.

Session 4: Sharing Myths

Getting Ready

1. Choose a wall for display of student drawings, arranged, as possible, near the picture of phenomena they seek to explain.

2. If appropriate, have student masks available for dramatizing the student stories.

Sharing the Students' Stories

1. Have the class imagine it's nighttime long ago and they are gathered around the fire.

2. Have a pair of volunteers tell their story and describe what the picture shows.

3. After everyone has shared, discuss the way that their story-explanations, based on observations of natural phenomena, are also inferences in that they seek to explain an observation.

4. Scientists try to explain their observations with inferences too, and keep testing them and modifying as necessary.

Sharing How the Stars Came to Be

1. Depending on age level and background, emphasize that Native Americans include many diverse nations and tribes. They are peoples of the present, as well as being the original inhabitants of this part of the world.

2. You may also want to stress that while Native American stories are wonderful and powerful, they are far from the only ways that they, or other peoples with ancient roots, look at the world, and their accomplishments in numerous field, including science and mathematics, are many. Provide additional background as needed.

3. Tell the class you'd like to share a story with them, and they should listen carefully to see what its lessons are, and what it could tell us about the people who created it.

4. Read/tell the story: "How the Stars Came to Be."

Mythology: Finding Clues to the Past

1. Ask for class reactions to the story.

2. Encourage all responses. As appropriate discuss: how the story constitutes evidence while the guesses about the people who told it are infereneces; how certain can we be of varying inferences and why?

3. Explain that anthropologists study myths and make inferences about the people who told them.

4. If there is time, share another story or stories, perhaps one told by the Native inhabitants of your region of the country. Discuss possible inferences about the people who told it. What other ways are there to find out whether an inference is supported by evidence?

5. Focus the class on their own stories. What might a future anthropologist infer about them from their stories?

Session 5: Uncovering the Past or What's Hidden in the Midden

Getting Ready
Before the Day of the Activity

1. Read through the session, paying particular attention to the preparation guidelines and various options described.

2. Begin collecting materials for the middens, including sending a letter home, and, if possible, arrange to have assistance in assembling the middens.

2. Decide how many layers you want to make, and how you want to arrange the middens.

4. Consider possible extensions and how they might affect the way you present the activities.

Getting Ready
On the Day of the Activity

1. Have demonstration materials for the role play and modelling of three main tasks available.

2. Decide how you want to organize teams of students.

Stepping Back in Time: An Introductory Role-Play

1. Have three volunteers help you dramatize the way that objects from the past can be buried.

2. During the role-play, ask students to describe some natural ways that objects might be buried. Ask where the oldest objects are most likely to be buried [in the deepest layers].

Introducing the Activity: Jobs of the Archaeologists

1. Put up the picture of the Midden Site and ask students to imagine the earth on the tray is a hillside. Define a midden as a place in an ancient village where objects have been left and buried over time.

2. Explain that archaeologists study the objects peoples of the past have left behind, often digging through layers of earth in middens to find artifacts.

3. Archaeologists work carefully and are respectful of past civilizations.
Write the three main tasks as: Excavators/Map Makers/Curators and explain and demonstrate their work.

4. Emphasize careful and patient work. Students will work in teams of three. They can share the main tasks by taking turns.

5. Have the teams of three cover their tables with newspaper and hand out the Archaeological Checklist Task Cards as appropriate. The team's Curator comes to pick up the midden when the team is ready to begin.

The Activity: Digging into the Past

1. Circulate among teams, carrying a container to remove the excavated soil. Emphasize that Excavators should go slowly, and explore laterally.

2. As appropriate, remind Map Makers to make a new map for each new layer.

3. Have each group make sure their names are on the maps and egg cartons. Explain that in the next session the class will discuss what they have found.

Session 6: Putting Together Clues from the Past

Getting Ready

1. Have maps and egg cartons ready for the discussion.

2. Decide the most appropriate way for your class to summarize and analyze the findings.

Discussing What Was Hidden in the Middens

1. Give student groups a few minutes to re-examine and discuss their finds.

2. Begin a class discussion by encouraging students to talk about their discoveries, controversies, surprises. How did it feel to be like archaeologists, working together on a project?

3. Use a chalkboard listing or pocket chart to list the different kinds of artifacts collected.

Artifact and Inference

1. Have students suggest possible uses for the different kinds of artifacts. Write these as headings, such as Food, Cookware, Clothing, Housing, etc.

2. Ask students to infer what uses specific objects may have had. Some objects may be in more than one category.

3. Ask: "If we pretend that the middens were real, what we guess about the lives, customs, eating habits, and environment of the people who left the items behind?"

4. Explain that archaeologists often disagree. Encourage students to discuss whether a particular inference seems farfetched or, on the other hand, seems supported by observable evidence.

Focusing on a Single Artifact

1. Ask students to select one artifact from their team's "museum" to sketch and write about. Have them list some of the inferences they can make about the object, and draw a picture of how people might have used it in the past.

2. After students finish their artifact reports, convene the class to share them, or display them so everyone can see.

Consider selecting "Going Further" activities for each of the sessions, as outlined in the text, and/or "Going Further" ideas for the entire unit, as listed on page 68.

S U N

MOON

S T A R S

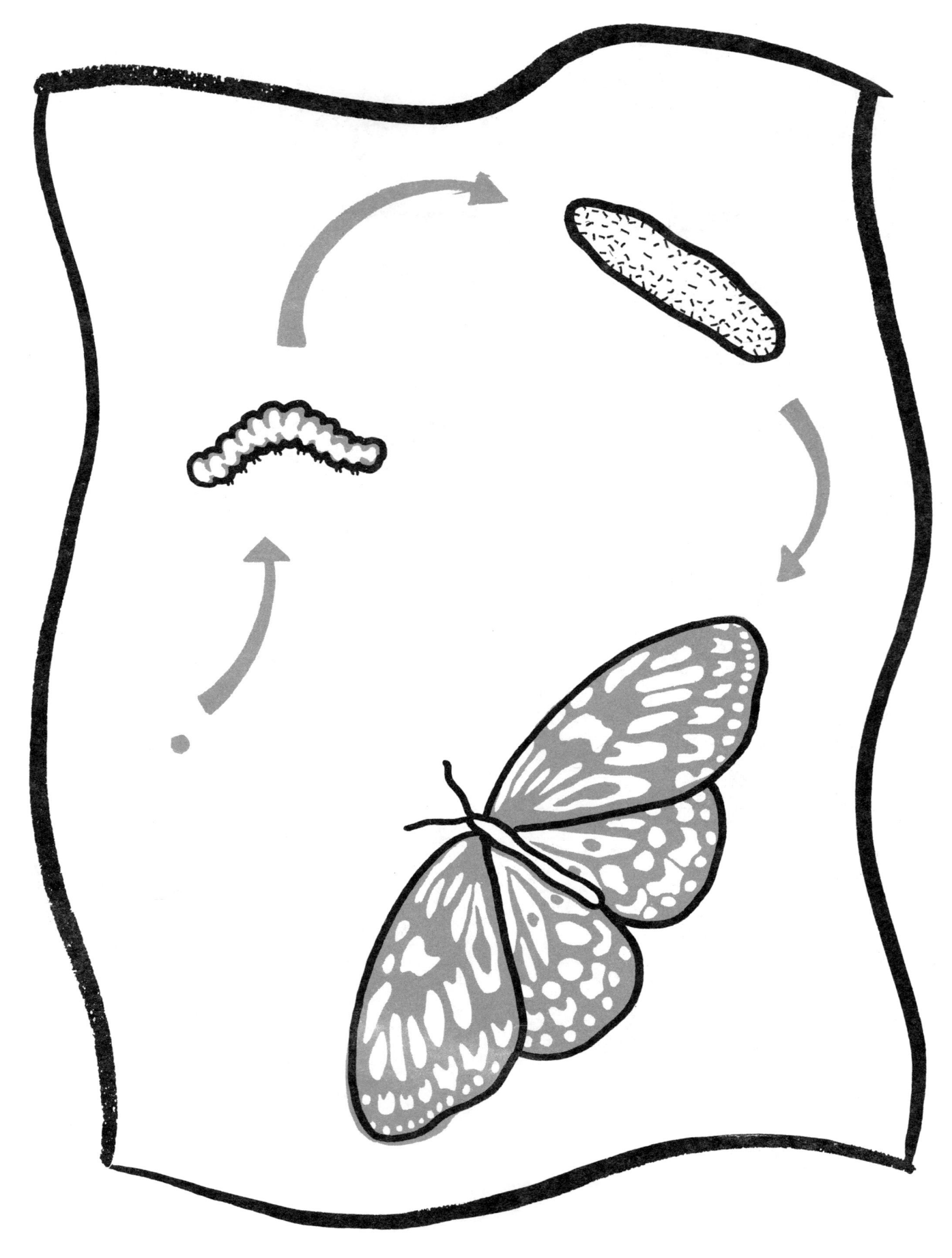

B U T T E R F L Y

R A I N B O W

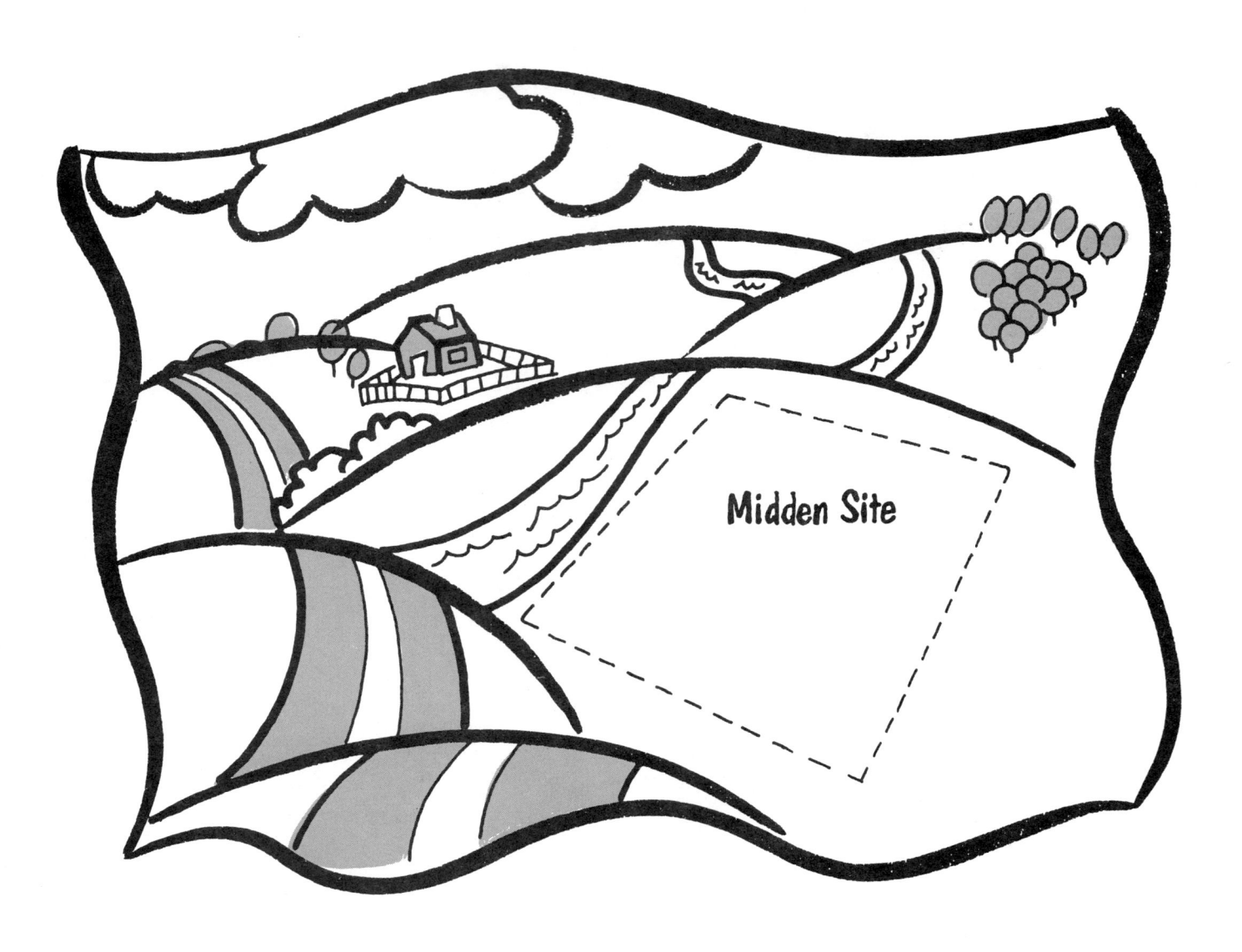

MIDDEN SITE

1 NORTHEAST CULTURE AREA
2 SOUTHEAST CULTURE AREA
3 GREAT PLAINS CULTURE AREA
4 NORTHWEST COAST CULTURE AREA
5 THE PLATEAU CULTURE AREA
6 GREAT BASIN CULTURE AREA
7 CALIFORNIA CULTURE AREA
8 SOUTHWEST CULTURE AREA

NOTE:
This map provides a general sense of where Native peoples lived prior to European contact. Locations are approximate and differed over time. The map shows only some of the hundreds of distinct groupings, tribes, and/or nations. Exact tribal designations and spelling differ from source to source. It is estimated that, in 1492, from two to ten million people lived in North America, with estimates for North and South America together ranging from 15 to 60 million people. At that time, in North America alone, 300 distinct cultures and over 200 different languages had been developed. It is recommended that you obtain larger maps and other resources to help your class become more aware of Native America past and present, such as a more detailed map of your region, showing tribal location, as well as lingustic and cultural groups. We adapted and modified our map from several sources, including Atlas of the North American Indian and Keepers of the Animals (both listed in the references), as well as maps from the U.S. Geological Survey and the National Geographic Society. ●

ARCHAEOLOGIST CHECKLIST TASK CARDS
Check the Tasks and Tools

✂ •

Check the Tasks You Do and Tools You Use _____ (name)

Excavator:

    ❏   Carefully remove soil layer by layer

    ❏   Tell Map Maker when you find an object

    ❏   Remove sifted soil to dump bag

Tools:

    ❏   Spoon

    ❏   Brush

    ❏   Sifter

✂ •

Check the Tasks You Do and Make a Map _____ (name)

Map Maker:

    ❏   Make a map of the Midden box

    ❏   Draw or trace each object on the map

    ❏   Write the name of the object

Midden Map

Shell

Bone

Wood

✂ •

Check the Tasks You Do and Tools You Use _____ (name)

Museum Curator:

    ❏   Help the Map Maker decide where to draw an object

    ❏   Clean off each object found

    ❏   Group similar objects in the egg carton

Tools:

    ❏   Cleaning Brush

    ❏   "Museum"